NEW MEXICO

Also by Patrick Lavin

Arizona: An Illustrated History

The Celtic World: An Illustrated History

The Navajo Nation: A Visitor's Guide
(WITH JOAN LAVIN)

NEW MEXICO
An Illustrated History

Patrick Lavin

Hippocrene Books, Inc.

New York

For information, address:
  HIPPOCRENE BOOKS, INC.
  171 Madison Avenue
  New York, NY 10016
  www.hippocrenebooks.com

Library of Congress Cataloging-in-Publication Data

  Lavin, Patrick.
    New Mexico : an illustrated history / Patrick Lavin.
      p. cm.
    Includes bibliographical references and index.
  ISBN-13: 978-0-7818-1053-1 (alk. paper)
  ISBN-10: 0-7818-1053-1
      1. New Mexico—History. 2. New Mexico—History—Pictorial works.
  I. Title.

  F796.L28 2007
  978.9—dc22   2007039600

Printed in the United States of America.

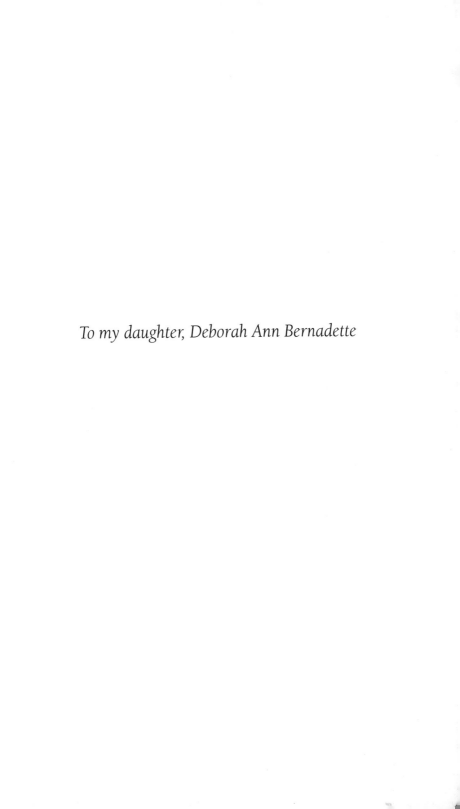

To my daughter, Deborah Ann Bernadette

Acknowledgments

Writing this history of New Mexico would have been an arduous, if not an unrealizable, task had it not been for the support and encouragement of many individuals.

I am, first of all, grateful to my wife, Joan, who devoted many long hours scrutinizing the manuscript: her piercing eye combed every word for accuracy and definition, and her creative suggestions substantially enhanced and clarified the text.

A *special muchas gracias* must go to my daughter Edie, whose reading of the entire manuscript wrought many constructive revisions that helped immeasurably in shaping the final outcome.

There were others, of course, who contributed in more or less measure and whose help I acknowledge with gratitude: Anita Martinez, Mike Whalen, Dick Mann, Claire Mather, Jerry Lujan, and the people at Hippocrene Books, Inc., especially my editors.

The many historians and writers I consulted will be evident throughout the book and are acknowledged in the bibliography.

In conclusion, of course, I accept full responsibility for any inaccuracies that may have crept into the text, despite careful scrutiny by the editors and others.

Contents

Introduction

This concise history of New Mexico aims at an all-inclusive treatment of the chain of historical events from the arrival of the Paleo-Indians to the post–World War II era. The story is centered on the contributions of New Mexico's three peoples—Indian, Spanish, and Anglo—who have learned to work together and prosper, often in the face of great challenges.

Appropriately, the history of New Mexico begins with the peoples who discovered the area before the first Europeans arrived in the sixteenth century. While New Mexico may be relatively young, as its name indicates, it has been home for countless peoples who have dwelt in its valleys, canyons, and mountains for generations. We have little information about these ancient colonists and can only guess about their cultures, social characteristics, and forms of social organization. Prehistoric societies left few records other than the bones of the large animals they hunted. Consequently, historians have had to rely almost entirely on archaeological evidence to piece together the obscure roots and living styles of these ancient peoples. What we do know is that they moved as nomadic bands across the southwestern landscape in response to the rhythm of the seasons and the availability of food.

People of an unknown type, described by archaeologists as Sandia people, left the earliest sign of human existence in what is now New

1

Mexico. Following them were the Clovis people, named for the site where artifacts established their presence in the area some nine to ten thousand years ago. The discovery of bison bones and fluted projectile points near Folsom, in northeastern New Mexico, presented evidence that a culture or group described by archaeologists as Folsom people lived and hunted in the area some eight to nine thousand years ago. Other cultures followed. Some, such as the Mogollon and Hohokam peoples, survived for generations and then mysteriously disappeared. Others, such as the Anasazi culture and the speakers of the Athabaskan language family, evolved into more highly developed groups. By the close of the first millennium, Anasazi societal progress had reached the zenith of its development: the settlers moved from pit houses and relocated to the tops of mesas, where they built huge cliff dwellings consisting of lofty apartment-type structures. At Chaco Canyon, they built a complex system of roads, some enormous, extending in several directions to other villages or ceremonial centers.

When the Spaniards arrived in the sixteenth century, they found a variety of Native American tribes within the present borders of the state of New Mexico. These varied from the sedentary Pueblos, grouped together in tightly integrated communities, to simple nomadic tribes still in the primitive food-gathering stage. The Pueblos, descendants of the Anasazi culture, lived in multistoried adobe villages, where they raised domestic animals and crops. They developed extensive and elaborate irrigation and water-conservation systems, similar to those of their Anasazi ancestors. The Pueblos also had a complex interrelated framework of governmental social and religious organizations, with religion so central to their lives that many historians describe their form of government as theocratic.

New Mexico's second discoverers were Spanish soldiers eager to find new lands to conquer and wealth to claim. With the soldiers came zealous men of God, who were "as determined as any soldier to conquer in the name of the cross they bore."[1] Out of this quest came the exploration and ultimate conquest of the land that they would call *Nueva México*.

---

1. Fergusson, *New Mexico*, p. 135.

The first exploration of New Mexico came in 1540, less than fifty years after Columbus set foot on an obscure island in the Caribbean. Spain's success in Mexico and Chile prompted new explorers to be on the alert for lands that might prove as wealthy. The circulating story of the mysterious "Seven Golden Cities of Cibola," located somewhere in the trackless wastelands of northern Mexico, lured the Spaniards northward. In 1540, Francisco Vásquez de Coronado set out from Mexico City to find these cities. Instead, he found the multistoried stone and mud Indian village of Hawikuh. Notwithstanding his failure to find the treasure he sought, history records his expedition as a journey of epic proportions. In little more than two years, Coronado and his men explored much of the Southwest. They ventured deep into the plains of Kansas, discovered the Grand Canyon, and visited all the major Native American villages in the future New Mexico territory.

For nearly forty years after Coronado returned home, the region that would become Nueva México was all but forgotten. In the meantime, however, the Spaniards, long obsessed with finding treasure, had not given up on their dream of finding the elusive Seven Golden Cities of Cibola. But riches and mythical legends were not the only inducements luring the Spaniards northward. There was also the strong missionary zeal, the determination to save the souls of the heathen native inhabitants.

To lead the first ambitious undertaking of colonizing New Mexico, the viceroy of New Spain selected Don Juan de Oñate, whose father Don Cristóbal had helped Hernando Cortés conquer Mexico earlier in the century. In 1598, Oñate organized and led the first *entrada* of Spaniards into the harsh unknown land peopled by hostile natives. During the next several decades, a string of Spanish settlements was established along the Rio Grande from Socorro in the south to the Taos Valley in the north. However, New Mexico grew slowly.

The seventeenth century presented a series of challenges to Spanish rule in New Mexico. Spanish intolerance of Pueblo religious practices and a persistent abuse of Native American labor prompted several futile revolts during this period. The crisis reached its peak in 1675 when forty-three Pueblo *caciques* (priests) were arrested and charged with practicing sorcery and plotting to rebel against the Spaniards. Several religious leaders were hanged and the others severely beaten. This led to the uprising in 1680, when several thousand Pueblo warriors converged on Santa Fe, laying siege to the city. In the battle that followed, four hundred colonists were killed and the governor and more than one thousand Spaniards were forced to flee the territory.

Spanish authorities reconquered most of New Mexico's Pueblos in 1692, but a further rebellion occurred in 1696. For the next several years, New Mexico suffered intensely from incessant hostility. The Spaniards eventually got the upper hand, and the Pueblos made peace. This led to more Spanish families settling in the territory. Missions were reestablished and, by the start of the eighteenth century, a new era had begun.

The history of New Mexico in the eighteenth century is that of bitter, and sometimes brutal, conflict between church and state for supremacy. In general, the issues in this controversy grew out of the conflict of religious and economic motives that existed in all of colonial Spanish America, one of which was the gross mistreatment of the Native Americans. It was more bitter in New Mexico than elsewhere; isolation made it unrealistic to enforce Spanish laws relative to the treatment of the native inhabitants, and also because in the poverty-stricken land, native labor was virtually the only source of wealth available for exploitation.

As the nineteenth century got underway, the closing stage of Spain's precarious hold on New Mexico was fast approaching. Mexico gained its independence from Spain in 1821, bringing to a close three centuries of Spanish rule on the North American continent. At the same time, New Mexico became part of the Mexican Republic. The most notable of the changes that came about with the change of government was the termination of Spanish policies that restricted contact with foreigners. This protectionist policy was replaced by a new policy that encouraged open trade with the outside, especially with Anglo-Americans. The event most worthy of mention in this period occurred in 1836, when the Mexican government dispatched Albino Pérez to New Mexico to assume the post of governor. The Pérez administration met immediate opposition, and the protest quickly escalated into a full-scale revolt. Badly equipped, the Pérez militia force was overwhelmed, and Pérez was captured and beheaded. The short-lived revolt of 1837 came to a bloody end when a squadron of dragoons from Mexico arrived at Santa Fe in January 1838.

Politically, New Mexico was a province until 1824, when its status changed to that of a territory. In 1836, it became a department and remained so until the end of Mexican rule.

The quarter century of Mexican rule in New Mexico ended in 1846. The United States Congress declared war with Mexico on May 13, 1846. Three months later, General Stephen Watts Kearny and his Army of the West marched along the Santa Fe Trail into New Mexico's undefended northern frontier. He took Santa Fe without firing a shot, instituted the Kearny Code (a new set of laws under which New Mexico was to be governed), and appointed Charles Bent as the first civil governor. While Kearny and his aides organized a new government in the ancient Spanish capital, secret plans were being hatched to oust the Yankee conquerors. A revolt occurred in 1847, and, after a furious two-day battle, the insurrection was crushed.

The war with Mexico ended when the Treaty of Guadalupe Hidalgo was signed in 1848. Two years later, the United States Congress passed an Organic Act that created the Territory of New Mexico and authorized the establishment of a new civil government. As established by Congress, New Mexico consisted of present-day New Mexico, Arizona, parts of southern Colorado, southern Utah, and even a portion of southeast Nevada, boundaries retained until 1861.

New Mexico played a small but significant role in the Civil War. The most important encounter of that war in New Mexico occurred at Apache Canyon east of Santa Fe in 1862, which ended with a victory for the Union side. After the Civil War, Washington turned its attention to containing New Mexico's hostile Native American tribes. To achieve this purpose, the army waged a merciless war against all Navajo and Apache tribes, forcing them to their knees and then confining them to reservations. By 1880, most of New Mexico's Native Americans had been relegated to reservations.

In the years following the Civil War, New Mexico underwent a period of unparalleled growth, much of which was attributable to the arrival of the railroads and the development of the cattle industry. When Texas cattlemen discovered the lush grama grass pastures along the Rio Grande, they moved in with their herds.

The area's growth and economic development brought problems. As the territory grew, so did lawlessness and regional conflicts that were often complicated by political and commercial rivalries. Violence on the western frontier was rampant in the latter part of the nineteenth century. Farmers and ranchers, cattlemen and sheepmen, and a variety of opposing groups engaged in frequent feuds, either over their neighbors' possessions or against their neighbors. The Lincoln County War in southeastern New Mexico, a conflict with many factions warring against one another, is ranked as one of the most notable conflicts of the American frontier and lasted from 1878 to 1881.

The road from territorial status to statehood was protracted and difficult. New Mexicans patiently endured sixty-two years of territorial status before the long-awaited ambition of becoming an integral part of the United States was finally achieved. In the interim, no other state had as many setbacks or fought so vigorously to be admitted to the Union as New Mexico. Numerous reasons have been given as to why it took more than half a century to achieve statehood. According to many, statehood was opposed by those who felt that New Mexico's predominantly Hispanic and Native American populations were too foreign and too Catholic for equal partnership in the Union. There were questions about the loyalty of these recently conquered peoples toward their new country. Despite the myriad of racial, religious, political, and economic issues, which delayed every attempt at statehood, New Mexico was admitted as a state on January 6, 1912.

Any lingering questions about loyalty were finally put to rest when New Mexicans demonstrated their patriotism during World War II and fulfilled their obligations to the war effort, earning a significant number of Congressional Medals of Honor. Grateful Americans recall the unique role one group of New Mexicans played in the war effort—the Navajo code breakers, who, under the guidance of the military, perfected a special code using their native language to transmit vital battle messages that the Japanese were unable to decipher. In recognition of their dedicated service to the United States, the Navajo code talkers were awarded a Certificate of Appreciation from President Reagan in

December 1981. A movie, *The Wind Talkers*, released in 2002, pays tribute to the war effort of the Navajo code breakers.

The arrival of the railroads in the late nineteenth century ended the centuries of isolation that New Mexico had endured from the time Europeans first reached it in the sixteenth century. The railroads made it easier for settlers to move to the territory and acquire land, and the population grew. However, New Mexico's most important economic upturn did not occur until the onset of World War II, when national defense found the state's vast open spaces and its emerging urban areas attractive for military training and weapons research. At Los Alamos, the top-secret Manhattan Project was conducted under the direction of J. Robert Oppenheimer. The result was the first atomic explosion (code name Trinity) at Alamogordo, 210 miles south of Los Alamos, on July 16, 1945. The Manhattan Project created the Los Alamos National Laboratory, which is at the forefront of international scientific development, as well as the Sandia National Laboratories in Albuquerque.

New Mexico advertises itself as the "Land of Enchantment," to which its magnificent landscapes and sweeping vistas readily attest. Its alluring terrain and its varied native population, many of whom still practice the rites of prehistoric Native Americans and Europeans of the Middle Ages, beckon modern-day explorers to discover its treasures. One such discoverer was the novelist D. H. Lawrence, who penned the following:

> The moment I saw the brilliant, proud morning shine high over the deserts of Santa Fe, something stood still in my soul. . . . In the magnificent fierce morning of New Mexico one sprang awake, a new part of the soul woke up suddenly, and the old world gave way to a new.[2]

---

2. Bartlett, *Familiar Quotations*, p. 940.

CHAPTER ONE

Land of Enchantment

The river that most fully exemplifies New Mexico and all the people who have made it is the fabled, historic, and forever undependable Rio Grande.

—Erna Fergusson, *New Mexico: A Pageant of Three Peoples*

New Mexico—"Land of Enchantment" to its residents—is an alluring land where lofty mountain peaks provide a spectacular backdrop for unrivaled terrain. Few individuals have described it more fittingly than native daughter Erna Fergusson:

Mountain ranges, tending generally north and south, divide the waters which will reach the Gulf of Mexico through the Rio Grande and the streams which led the pioneers across Texas, and those which the Colorado and the Gila will carry to the Gulf of California. Between the ranges, the valleys. Some are narrow, with ever flowing streams and fertile with humus from the slopes. Some are vast alkali flats, wind-eroded deserts, or stretches of wavering grass. . . . Toward the main streams, canyons fan out onto the floors of the great valleys; away from the rivers, they flatten down onto dun-colored plains.[1]

---

1. Fergusson, *Our Southwest*, p. 246.

GEOGRAPHICAL DIMENSIONS

New Mexico, with its 121,598 square miles of territory, ranks as the fifth largest state in the Union, after Alaska, Texas, California, and Montana. It is positioned between 103 and 109 degrees west longitude, and 31 and 37 degrees north latitude. It measures 370 miles from north to south, and 343 miles from east to west. It has no natural boundaries; its borders were created by several measures enacted by Congress during its territorial period. Colorado lies along the full extent of its northern border, Texas and the western tip of Oklahoma border are on the east, Texas and the Republic of Mexico are on its southern border, and Arizona borders its western side. It joins Utah (along with Colorado and Arizona) at the spot known as Four Corners.

TOPOGRAPHICAL FEATURES

New Mexico's terrain is as diverse as its people. In some parts of the state, snowcapped mountains thrust toward the heavens with all of their majestic beauty, while in other areas there are vast arid regions where even cacti struggle to stay alive. New Mexico belongs to four U.S. physiographic provinces (an area delineated according to similar terrain that has been shaped by a common geologic history).

The Great Plains Province, embracing the eastern third of the state, consists of the *Llano Estacado* (Staked Plains) with some of the flattest land found anywhere. Interesting saucer-like depressions, varying in diameter from more than a few yards to several miles, are found in the Llano Estacado. Near Raton (in the northeast of this province) is Capulin Mountain, which rises to an elevation of 8,182 feet. At its upper level is a volcanic cinder cone one thousand feet tall with a crater some four hundred feet deep at the summit. It was formed about 2,300 years ago in the last great period of volcanic activity in western North America.

The Southern Rocky Mountains Province, covering the north-central area, is where the Rockies extend to a point just south of Santa

Fe. This is the highest and most rugged part of the state. Mountain streams, coniferous forests, snowcapped peaks, and deep river canyons make this an area of great scenic beauty. The Sangre de Cristo Mountain Range marks the eastern edge of this province.

The Colorado Plateau Province has two sections in New Mexico: the Navajo and the Datil. The Navajo section takes its name from the Indian reservation that occupies the extreme northwestern corner of the state. The distinctive features of the landscape are young plateaus, rock terraces, and mesas. The San Juan River and the Chuska Mountains fall within this section. The Datil section, lying directly south of the Navajo, is an area covered with lava and volcanic necks (columns of igneous rock).

The Basin and Range Province covers the southwest and central portions of the state and embraces the Mexican Highlands and the Sacramentos.[2] The principal mountain ranges in the Mexican Highland section are the Sandia and Manzano mountains east of Albuquerque, the San Andreas Mountains between Socorro and Las Cruces and the Mogollon Mountains near the Arizona border. The Sacramento section covers an area some three hundred miles long and seventy miles wide in the south-central part of the state. Among its mountain ranges are the Jicarilla, Sierra Blanca, Sacramento, and Guadalupe. To the south is White Sands near Alamogordo, where gypsum from surrounding mountains dissolves and washes into the basin below, creating white dunes some thirty to forty feet high.

LIFE ZONES

Few areas in the world the size of New Mexico offer such a broad range of life zones—six in all—as well as the native plants and animals that inhabit them. At the lower end of the life zones is the Lower Sonoran, where altitudes are usually below 4,500 feet. This life zone

---

2. The physiographic subdivisions are taken from Beck, *New Mexico: A History of Four Centuries*, pp. 3–9, which references Nevin M. Fenneman, *Physiography of the Western United States*.

The Rio Grande River with Sandia Mountains in the background.
(PHOTO BY T. HARMON PARKHURST)

embraces an area of 19,500 square miles in the Rio Grande valley below Socorro, in the Pecos Valley up to Santa Rosa and in most of the southwestern part of the state. This is the most important agricultural zone, primarily because of its long frost-free period, fertile soil, and higher temperatures. Its plant life includes mesquite, cactus, valley cottonwood, and black grama grass.

The Upper Sonoran, embracing the plains, foothills, and valleys lying above 4,500 feet, covers about 79,600 square miles, or two-thirds of the entire state. There is considerable variation in the vegetation of this zone because it covers such a vast region. At the lower altitudes, vegetation is very sparse, due to the prevailing arid conditions. Blue grama and buffalo grass, piñon, juniper, and some trees are found at the higher elevations, the obvious result of higher rainfall.

The Transition is the major timber zone, where Ponderosa and scrub oak are the most common trees. This zone is found on the middle mountain slopes of the high ranges at altitudes of 7,000 to 8,500 feet on the northeast slopes and 8,000 to 9,500 feet on the southwest slopes. It covers an area of about 19,000 square miles.

The Canadian is the zone of the aspen, blue spruce, and Douglas fir. It lies at altitudes of 8,500 to 12,000 feet and embraces an area of 4,000 square miles. Its rain or snowfall feeds the streams that irrigate the more arid regions.

The Hudsonian zone occurs in a narrow scrubby timberline belt around the higher peaks, above 11,000 feet. It covers only 160 square miles, and its only commercial use is summer pasture for sheep.

The Artic-Alpine is the treeless zone above 12,000 feet elevation. It is found as a cap on the highest peaks and is important only because it frequently retains snow until late summer, when it is most needed in the dry valleys below.[3]

Wheeler Peak, near Taos, rises to an altitude of 13,160 feet, the highest point in the state. The lowest elevation is in the southern part of the state: Red Bluff on the Pecos, south of Carlsbad, has an altitude of less than 3,000 feet. Eighty-five percent of the state has an altitude greater than 4,000 feet.

---

3. The basic source of this section is Beck, pp. 9–10, referring to Vernon Bailey, *Life Zones and Crop Zones of New Mexico*.

RIVERS

Historically, water has played a crucial role in the growth of New Mexico. Until improved technology made the exploration of ground water possible in the early twentieth century, man's use of New Mexico's resources was largely limited to the valleys of the five main rivers: Rio Grande, Pecos, Canadian, San Juan, and Gila. If they knew where water could be found, nomadic Indians occasionally lived in the arid areas.

The Rio Grande River, third longest river in the United States, is the fullest embodiment of New Mexico and its people. From its source in southwestern Colorado until it empties into the Gulf of Mexico (near Brownsville, Texas), the Rio Grande travels some 1,800 miles, most of it through the very heart of New Mexico. The Pecos River lies east of the Rio Grande and follows a course approximately parallel to it. East of the Pecos there are no mountains, just high plains that break down to a steep escarpment, known for a hundred miles or more as Cap Rock.

The Canadian River rises on the eastern slope of the Sangre de Cristo Mountains. It follows a course through the Llano Estacado and beyond, through Oklahoma and Arkansas from where it flows into the Mississippi. The San Juan River surfaces in Colorado and then swings a generous loop into New Mexico through the Navajo's rolling desert before heading north again to join the Colorado. The source of the Gila River is in the high Mogollon and Black Range mountains of southwestern New Mexico; the Gila flows in a southwesterly direction across Grant and Hidalgo counties before reaching the Arizona border. In states of the eastern United States, navigation played a vital role during the early history, but the same cannot be said about New Mexico. None of the rivers were navigable, and, according to early adventurers, the Rio Grande could not even be navigated by canoe.

STATE CAPITAL

Santa Fe is the state capital. Established in 1610, it is both the oldest city in the state and the oldest state capital in the United States.

Located in a valley surrounded by snowcapped mountain peaks, its attractive natural setting is enhanced by its historical allure. The flags of Spain, Mexico, the Confederacy, and the United States have at different times flown over the city. Its distinctive architecture and unique atmosphere have made Santa Fe a magnet for tourists.

DEMOGRAPHICS

New Mexico's population reached 1,819,046 at the beginning of the twenty-first century. Whites, of non-Hispanic origin, made up 45 percent of the population. Hispanics composed slightly more than 41 percent, while Native Americans represented 9.5 percent.[4]

---

4. Data derived from Population Estimates, 2000 Census of Population (www. quickfacts.census.gov/gfd/states).

CHAPTER TWO

Pre-European Peoples

If any people belong entirely to New Mexico it has to be the Pueblo people, a culture with roots reaching back to the pre-historic Anasazi or "Basket People."

—Erna Fergusson, *New Mexico: A Pageant of Three Peoples*

Millenniums ago, Asiatic people began migrating across the Bering Strait onto the American continent and, over time, worked their way southward and eastward. According to archaeological findings, New Mexico has been inhabited from as early as twelve thousand years ago—a rough estimate, as prehistoric man left few footprints from which to make a conclusive calculation. The first known inhabitants of the Southwest, referred to in archeological terms as Paleo-Indians, were the mammoth hunters; as the environment changed and the big game they hunted moved eastward, they followed. As they withdrew, bands from the western desert regions and from present-day northern Mexico moved into the areas they vacated.

Archeologists tell of an unknown type they describe as Sandia people (from prehistoric remains found at Sandia Cave near Albuquerque) as having left the earliest clue of human existence in what is now New Mexico. Following them were the Clovis people, named for the site where artifacts (found in 1932) established their presence in the area some eleven thousand years ago. Little is known about them except that they were big-game hunters who topped their spears with sharp, chipped spear points of stone.[1] About a thousand years later, a culture or group described by archeologists as Folsom people roamed

---

1.   Fergusson, *New Mexico: A Pageant of Three Peoples*, page 15.

Black Cowboy George McJunkin on "Headless" (1911).

the American Southwest. The first evidence of this culture surfaced in 1908 with the discovery of bison bones and fluted projectile points in an arroyo near present-day Folsom in northeastern New Mexico. George McJunkin, a black cowboy, was riding up Wild Horse Gulch when he came upon the find. Investigated by archeologists years later, the bones proved to be those of the extinct giant bison. Together with the Folsom projectile points, they provided proof that man had lived and hunted in New Mexico eight to ten thousand years ago.[2]

---

2.   Roberts, *A History of New Mexico*, p. 21.

Over the next four thousand or so years, a new culture—identified as Desert people—evolved on the west side of the Continental Divide. The people of this culture operated an economy based on the collecting of wild foods and the hunting of small game. Some time later, they added *maíz* (Indian corn or maize) and other food vegetables to supplement their diet. (Primitive ears of corn, dating between 3,000 and 2,500 BC, were excavated at Bat Cave in west-central New Mexico in 1949.) Because many of their sites have been located in Cochise territory, these desert dwellers are grouped together as the Cochise people. Archeologists characterize them as the link between the ancient mammoth hunters and the new, more precocious cultures that began emerging in the Southwest around 300 BC. The most important of the cultures to emerge in the post-Cochise era were, in archeological terms, the Mogollon, Anasazi, and Hohokam. The people from the Mogollon and Anasazi cultures were primarily located in present-day New Mexico. Those of the Hohokam culture were to the west in present-day Arizona.[3]

MOGOLLON CULTURE

The Mogollon culture, the first of the post-Cochise era cultures, emerged some time around 300 BC and came into its own about 100 BC. A mountain people living on wild game, nuts, and berries, they ranged across southwestern New Mexico, eastern Arizona, and northern Mexico in the region that later became known as Apacheria. In the first centuries of the Christian era, these mountain dwellers became the dominant people of the Southwest; they lived in one-room pit house villages, worshiped in ceremonial lodges, farmed mesa tops, and produced ceramics of fine quality.[4]

Mogollon influence gradually spread northward to the Four Corners area, where New Mexico now meets Colorado, Utah, and Arizona. Scholars believe this culture reached its zenith about AD 1050 and then declined until it disappeared completely in the late 1200s.

---

3.   Simmons, *New Mexico: An Interpretive History,* p. 51.
4.   Ibid.

The cause for its disappearance is not clear. Archeologists attribute it to invading forces, others to adverse climatic conditions. Some scholars have theorized that the Mogollons migrated en masse to the Casa Grandes area of Chihuahua, Mexico. Along the Mimbres River in southwestern New Mexico was the Mimbres culture, believed to have been a branch of the Mogollon culture. Little is known of them, except for their distinctive pottery style, characterized by the intricate black or red animal figures they left behind. Archeologists suggest the Mimbres dropped out of sight about AD 1300, when adverse climatic conditions forced them northward. Over time, they assimilated with the Pueblo cultures of the upper Rio Grande.

Anasazi Culture

The Anasazi culture, next in the post-Cochise cultures (and the one that evolved into the Pueblo culture), developed more slowly than the Mogollon culture from the time it first appeared at the Four Corners area around 100 BC. Dubbed "Basket Makers" because of the delicate storage baskets they made from yucca fibers, the Anasazis had evolved from a nomadic to a sedentary lifestyle by the sixth century, cultivating crops of corn, beans, and squash. In the eighth century, they moved out of their caves into pit houses—cone-shaped, one-room structures built partially below ground. They replaced the *atlatl*[5] with the bow and arrow for hunting game, and they discovered the *mano*[6] for grinding corn into meal.

By the close of the first millennium, Anasazi societal progress was surpassing the older Mogollon culture. They relocated to the tops of mesas, where they built huge cliff communities consisting of lofty apartment-type dwellings. Some were enormous, containing hundreds of rooms. Pueblo Bonito in Chaco Canyon, New Mexico, was five stories high and had over eight hundred compartments.

---

5. A weapon that enabled the prehistoric Indian to throw a spear harder and farther than a hand-thrown weapon.

6. "Milling stone" or "hand mill." The *mano*, with its companion implement, the *meta*, was first used by the prehistoric Indians of the Southwest to grind corn and other kernels.

The Anasazi people built a complex system of roads extending from Chaco Canyon in several directions to other villages or ceremonial centers; one road extended for forty miles to the San Juan River. They improved their farming methods and developed an effective irrigation system for watering their fields. These and similar feats tell us that the Anasazi had evolved into a highly developed societal organization, one that could mobilize and coordinate the large labor crews such projects would have required.[7]

Archeologists maintain that the Anasazi culture reached the zenith of its progress during the first half of the twelfth century. A century and a half later, Chaco Canyon had become a ghost town. The Anasazi people had mysteriously abandoned their high-walled communities and migrated elsewhere: "They left with their great stone towns and kivas standing undamaged and unburned."[8] Archeologists disagree over what brought this migration about. Some believe the stimulus to abandonment was a catastrophic twenty-three-year drought; others suggest warfare, either from within the Anasazi culture or from outside invaders, but there is no evidence whatsoever of such warfare.

Where did the Anasazi move? Some drifted south and founded new communities at Zuni and Hopi. Most, however, drifted eastward in two successive migrations and settled in the valleys of the Rio Grande and its tributaries. Archeological studies show that settled agricultural people from large communities to the north and west moved into the Rio Grande valley during the last half of the 1200s. Continued movements of people from the west were still entering the Rio Grande valley shortly before the Spaniards arrived in the sixteenth century.[9]

The Spaniards came face-to-face with the descendants of the Anasazi along the 350-mile stretch of the Rio Grande and to the west at Acoma and Zuni. They were living in distinctively similar villages that were compactly built and often contained several two- and three-story houses. Their well-developed agriculture was enhanced by remarkable irrigation methods. They gave them the name "Pueblo" because

7. Simmons, *Interpretative History*, p. 52.
8. Greenberg, *The Tony Hillerman Companion*, p. 329.
9. Spicer, *Cycles of Conquest*, p. 153.

they lived in village communities not unlike the villages, or *pueblos*, back home.

In 1998, Chaco Canyon was proclaimed a World Heritage site by the United Nations, and the stone towns long abandoned by people known as Anasazi joined the great pyramids of Egypt, the Taj Mahal, the temples of Angkor Wat, and the majestic Mayan ruins at Copán as a world jewel.

HOHOKAM CULTURE

Further west in the Salt River Basin of western New Mexico (present-day southern Arizona), a third great post-Cochise culture evolved into a highly developed agriculture civilization that would last for 1,700 years before it mysteriously disappeared. They were the Hohokam—a present-day Pima Indian word meaning the "people who have gone." This agricultural society is believed to have migrated northward from Mexico around 300 BC and settled in villages along the Salt and Gila rivers. They had spread out and by AD 200 established communities along the Santa Cruz and Rillito rivers, where they lived in scattered villages. They met for ball games; made buff-colored pottery decorated with little figures of men, animals, and birds (believed to have been copied from Mimbres pottery); and they cremated their dead.[10] To grow crops in the arid desert, they modified their farming methods with a cleverly engineered canal irrigation system—a system that would serve as a model for twentieth-century irrigation projects in the area. Scholars who have studied the Hohokam culture call them the "first masters of the American desert."

With the onset of what is referred to as the Classic period, around AD 1150, Hohokams began to withdraw from outlying settlements and concentrate in large villages. Pit houses surrounding central plazas gave way to walled compounds. Casa Grande, the most impressive of the Hohokam structures, stands on the south bank of the Gila River near Coolidge, Arizona. On the north side of the Salt River, near the edge of the Phoenix airport, is Pueblo Grande, a building structure

---

10. Fergusson, *Our Southwest*, p. 116.

Aztec ruins, Aztec National Monument, NM (1961).

Zuni ruins, Zuni Pueblo, NM (1895).

Acoma Pueblo (1948).

Pueblo Bonito, Chaco Canyon, NM (1941).

Cliff Dwellings, Puyé, NM (1940). (PHOTO BY HAROLD KELLOGG)

outstripped in size and grandeur only by Casa Grande. According to archeologists, mirrors and copper bells taken from excavations at Casa Grande reveal a link to tropical Mexico, as do the shallow, oval pits found in major villages. These oval pits may have been arenas for ball games like the ones played by Aztecs, or they may have been gathering places for ceremonial activities of a religious nature.

During the first quarter of the fifteenth century, the Hohokam people mysteriously disappeared. One theory is that an epidemic may have wiped them out. The prevailing theory, however, is that alkalization of the soil caused by centuries of irrigation had made the land useless, forcing them to migrate elsewhere to survive. Before their demise, a people from the northeast moved into their land, although archeologists have uncovered no evidence that it was a warlike action; the two peoples seem to have lived affably together. The newcomers were the Salado people, who migrated south from the valley of the Little Colorado sometime between 1200 and 1350.[11]

Archeologists are still striving to unravel the great puzzle of where the Hohokams went, and why. Some believe they migrated south, probably into Mexico's great Chihuahua Basin—a claim that cannot be traced or validated. Others believe they were the ancestors of the modern Pima and Papago peoples. It is estimated they numbered fifteen thousand or more at the time of their disappearance. Whatever the fate of the Hohokam people, they will always be remembered in the Southwest for the incredible network of canals they left behind, which is an affirmation of their engineering mastery.

PUEBLO CULTURE

When the Spaniards arrived in the sixteenth century, they found the Pueblo people living in some sixty-five to seventy pueblos (villages) of similar character, averaging four hundred inhabitants and stretching northward along the Rio Grande River valley from Socorro to Taos and westward to Acoma and Zuni.

---

11. Ibid., p. 117.

The villages were compactly built, often with several two- or three-story houses. The communities were autonomous with no tribal political organization linking them into effective units larger than the individual villages. Each village was a tightly organized unit governed by its elders. A polytheistic religion, led by a priesthood and performed in a *kiva* (ceremonial chamber), played a meaningful role in the everyday life of the people. Coronado reported: "They do not have chiefs as in New Spain, but are ruled by a council of the oldest men. They have priests who . . . go up the highest roof of the village and preach from there, like criers in the morning while the sun is rising. . . . There is no drunkenness, no sodomy nor sacrifices, nor do they eat human flesh or steal, but they are generally at work."[12] Historian Edward H. Spicer states that the combined population of the villages when the Spaniards began to colonize the area was no more than forty thousand. The folk that occupied these villages were sedentary farmers who raised domestic animals for sustenance and had extensive and elaborate irrigation and water-conservation systems, not unlike those of their ancestors, the Anasazi. The Spaniards named them "Pueblo people."

While the different Pueblos enjoyed lifestyles that were similar in many ways, they spoke different languages. Four or five related languages, each with several dialects, existed. Spicer describes the language diversity as follows:

In the villages just north of El Paso the Spaniards heard a language spoken which bore no resemblance to the Indian languages of the south: the Spaniards called this Piro. It was in use in a half-dozen villages scattered through the valley for some hundred miles northward, to the vicinity of present-day Socorro, New Mexico. Adjoining on the north were twenty villages in which the people spoke a language the Spaniards came to call Tiwa. This resembled Piro somewhat, but immediately to the north were another seven villages speaking a totally differently language which had no similarity to Tiwa or Piro; these were the Keresan villages of which there were six

---

12. Ibid., p. 289.

in the Rio Grande Valley and another large one called Acoma fifty miles to the southwest.[13]

According to Spicer, a fifth distinct language—Tano—was spoken by the people of four villages in the Galisteo Basin east of the river, and north of these villages there were seven or more villages where the people spoke a language that the Spaniards called Tewa, which, although different from Tano, was intelligible to the Tanos. Bordering the Tanos on the east at Pecos were people whose language was quite different from that of the Keresans, Tanos, and Tewas. Spicer tells us the Towa language was also spoken by the people in eleven villages across the river to the west beyond the Keresans in the Jemez River valley. Beyond the Tewas, in two or more villages as far north as Taos, the Indians spoke a variety of Tiwa.[14]

In their quest for gold, the Spaniards journeyed into Pueblo territory for the first time in the 1500s. Probably the first clash between the white man and the New Mexico Pueblos occurred in 1540 when the Coronado expedition, having traveled from Mexico City north across the parched Chihuahuan Desert in search of the Seven Golden Cities of Cibola, arrived at a cluster of Zuni[15] villages near the present-day town of Gallup, New Mexico. There were six villages, the two largest being Hawikuh and Matsakya. Coronado's intrusion provoked a battle with the Zuni, who were defeated in the face of the Spaniards' superior armed force. Coronado's men seized the village and captured the food supply. The Zunis fled and took refuge on top of a mesa called Corn Mountain.

Coronado and his party next came face-to-face with Hopi Indians (also believed to have descended from the ancient Anasazi culture) in a place now called Jeddito Valley. Again, Coronado's intrusion into the Hopi village of Kawaiokuh provoked a skirmish. But the superior

---

13. Spicer, p. 153.
14. Ibid., pp. 152–153.
15. A story captioned "Major Prehistoric Southwestern Cultures" in the *Arizona Daily Star,* Monday, January 14, 2002, states that the Zuni claim kinship with the prehistoric Mogollon culture rather than with the ancient Anasazi.

Spaniards routed the Hopis and partly destroyed Kawaiokuh.[16] Coronado and his party eventually made contact with the eastern Pueblos of the Rio Grande valley, as they continued their journey.

Subsequent contacts with the Hopis took place in 1583 and again in 1598, when Governor Oñate sought and obtained their allegiance to the Spanish monarch. However, their isolation—two hundred miles from the center of Spanish administration in Santa Fe—spared them the cultural collision and change that the Pueblos along the Rio Grande would experience. The Hopis and the Zunis were the frontier people of New Mexico. As such, they were exempt from paying a tribute, required of the eastern Pueblos, for the upkeep of a garrison at Santa Fe.[17]

It is now accepted that the Pueblos either descended from the earlier Anasazi or that the Anasazis' lifestyle evolved in the direction of what has been called the Pueblo culture. In this regard, an intriguing archeological footnote is worth mentioning. In earlier studies archeologists had deduced, based on a striking difference in head shape, that the Pueblos were a different people who, at an earlier time, had conquered, or peacefully assimilated with, the Anasazi.[18] Further study revealed that the difference in head shape was brought about by the use of cradleboards, to which Pueblo infants were strapped for easy transportability. Prolonged resting of the infant's head on the hard board led to a flattening of the back of the skull, thus the prevailing head shape.

As discussed, the Anasazi-Pueblo culture in New Mexico reached its peak in the twelfth century with Chaco Canyon at the hub of a socioeconomic system that included some seventy outlying colonies connected by a network of roads.

ATHABASKAN LANGUAGE FAMILY

The largest groups of non-Pueblo Indians living in New Mexico are the Apaches and the Navajos. Both tribes belong to the Athabaskan

---

16. Spicer, p. 187.
17. Ibid., p. 190.
18. Fugate and Fugate, *Roadside History of New Mexico,* p. 169.

language family that also includes the Indians of Alaska and north-western Canada. Anthropologists and archeologists believe that both groups had lived in northwestern Canada before migrating south-ward many generations ago, but there is disagreement over when they settled in the New Mexico area. Some maintain that they arrived in the 1200s and may have been to blame for the abandonment by the Anasazi of their multistory cliff dwellings at Mesa Verde and Chaco Canyon. But there is no evidence that the Anasazis were driven away by hostile forces. Archeologists tell us they left at their leisure, leaving behind their great stone towns and kivas "undamaged and unburned."[19]

Historian Edward H. Spicer believes that the Athabaskans had been pushing southwestward from their northwestern habitant since the 1300s and were still in the process of this migration when the Spaniards arrived.[20] He also believes that as they pushed into the Southwest, they formed into bands and headed in different directions: the Navajo and Jicarilla Apache bands found a home in the San Juan River Basin of the Four Corners; the Mescalero Apache bands moved on to southern New Mexico; the Chiricahua Apache bands settled in northern Mexico, southern Arizona, and southwestern New Mexico; and those who became known as the western Apache were attracted to the rugged central mountains of Arizona. Little is known about these groups before the middle of the 1600s, except that their economic life was made up of bands with few fixed community locations. They practiced agriculture, along with hunting and wild-food gathering, but it was for them a secondary source of subsistence. It is believed there were as many as fifteen thousand Apaches and Navajos scattered throughout the region at the time the Spaniards arrived. According to Spicer, the Spaniards had almost no contact with either the Apaches or the Navajos until the early part of the 1600s. The Coronado party, when it visited New Mexico in 1540, encountered small groups of nomadic people, believed to have been the ancestors of the Navajos, in the country west of the Rio Grande Pueblo villages. Coronado had

19. Greenberg, p. 329.
20. Spicer, p. 14.

Navajo Indian baby in cradleboard. (COURTESY OF MARSHALL
TRIMBLE, DIRECTOR OF THE MARICOPA COMMUNITY COLLEGE SOUTHWEST
STUDIES PROGRAM)

"Na-buash-l-ta" Apache Medicine Man. (COURTESY OF MARSHALL TRIMBLE, DIRECTOR OF THE MARICOPA COMMUNITY COLLEGE SOUTHWEST STUDIES PROGRAM)

Apache Warrior. (COURTESY OF MARSHALL TRIMBLE, DIRECTOR OF THE MARICOPA COMMUNITY COLLEGE SOUTHWEST STUDIES PROGRAM)

heard stories from the Tano Pueblos in the Galisteo Basin about war-like Indians from the east who had been raiding the people of the area since at least 1525. Most historians believe that these raiders were most likely the ancestors of people the Spaniards would later name the Jicarilla and Mescalero Apaches.[21] However, there was no further contact with these warlike Indians until 1626, when Father Zarate-Salmerón learned from the Jemez Pueblos of people living to their north, whom they described as Apaches and "Navaju." An attempt was made to make contact with them. The next year the Franciscans opened a mission at Santa Clara, the Tewa village on the west side of the Rio Grande below San Juan, and began administering to them.[22]

The Apaches living on the eastern side of the Rio Grande would occasionally raid the Pueblo villages to the west during the early Spanish colonization period. During the revolt by the Pueblo Indians against their Spanish colonial overlords in 1680, the surrounding Athabaskan nomads avoided taking sides in the conflict. When the Spaniards reconquered the Pueblo communities in the late seventeenth century, the Athabaskans renewed raiding with greater intensity and frequency, hitting both Spanish and Pueblo communities. Over the next ten years, the frontier was in turmoil. By 1710 the Spaniards, unable to hold out against the raiding, sought a peaceful solution by coming to terms with the Indians.

During the 1700s the Spaniards succeeded in classifying several sub-groups among the southwestern Apaches. To the east were bands that ranged the headwaters of the Gila River and southward along the Mimbres River, becoming known to the Spaniards as the Mimbreños. Southwest of the Mimbreños, extending from about the present New Mexico–Arizona boundary to the valley of the San Pedro River, were groups who commanded the main corridors of Apache raiding in Sonora, whom the Spaniards called the Chiricahuas. (The Chiricahuas lived in New Mexico until their leader, Geronimo, surrendered to the U.S. military in 1886. Following the surrender, the Chiricahua were rounded up and transported to Florida, Alabama, and Oklahoma,

21. Ibid., p. 229.
22. Ibid., p. 14.

where they were held prisoner for the next twenty-seven years. Thereafter they were released to settlements in Oklahoma and the Mescalero Reservation in New Mexico, where the majority live today.) North of the Chiricahuas, ranging from the middle Gila River and its northern tributary, the San Carlos, were a number of different groups lacking unified leadership called the Pinaleños. North of the Pinaleños, from the Black River through the headwaters of the Salt River to the edge of the Mogollon Rim, lived what was probably the largest group, called the Coyoteros by the Spaniards. A fifth group lived northwest of the Coyoteros, from the Tonto Basin and the Mogollon Rim as far north as modern Flagstaff, and came to be known as the Tontos. The last three groups constituted the greater part of the western Apaches and were the least known to the Spaniards.[23]

Today, members of three tribes belonging to the Athabaskan-speaking peoples live in New Mexico. The largest, numbering more than 125,000, is the Navajo people. They are located on a reservation spread out across northwestern New Mexico, northeastern Arizona, and the southern tip of Utah. The second group consists of the Mescalero Apaches, who live east of the Rio Grande between Alamogordo and Roswell in south-central New Mexico. The third group, the Jicarilla Apaches, live west of the Rio Grande in the north-central part of the state.

NAVAJO

Before the Spaniards arrived, the Navajo were a small, insignificant tribe eking out a living from simple agriculture, supplemented by hunting, raiding, and gathering. Today, the Navajo people occupy Navajoland (*dine' bikeyah*), a reservation of some 16 million acres dominating northwestern New Mexico, much of northeastern Arizona, and the southern tip of Utah. Geographically, the area is awe-inspiring. In the words of writer Tony Hillerman, "Everywhere you look there are dramatic views of distant, angular mesas, expansive

---

23. Ibid., p. 244.

plateaus and wide, pale-green valleys. . . . In every direction the tree-less Navajo horizon stretches out before you in a landscape of tawny dunes, orange-and-pink canyons, and far away blue mountains rising more than 10,000 ft."[24]

Navajos have long been known for their ability to adapt to cultural and environmental changes. They have borrowed from all the people with whom they have been in contact. From the Spaniards they acquired sheep and horses and became some of the best herdsmen and horsemen in the Southwest. They also learned the art of silversmithing from the Spaniards. From the Hopis and the Pueblos, they acquired the skills of desert agriculture and weaving. They are renowned for their exquisite handwoven rugs.

Navajos believe they emerged from the underworld, the "first or black world"—a timeless place known only to the spirit-beings. It was also the place where First Man and First Woman lived, one in the east, the other in the west, before they were united after seeing each other's fire. As tradition describes it, First Man burned a crystal, symbolizing the awakening of the mind. First Woman then burned a piece of turquoise, and after four attempts the union was consummated.[25] Religion is the center of Navajo life. Despite efforts to Christianize them, they have continued to adhere to their own beliefs. They have religious rites for curing the sick, for sending the men off to war, and for many other situations and events. Their religion, with its masks, prayer plumes, nine-day ceremonies, and sacred meals, is full of Pueblo Indian lore and ceremonial art. There are many customs and taboos among the Navajo: the door of the *hogan* (house) must always face east; the Navajo must never kill a snake or a coyote, never eat bear meat; a Navajo man must never look at or speak to his mother-in-law even if he lives near her. When a person dies inside the hogan, the body is removed through a hole cut in the north wall and the hogan is not used again. The spirits or ghosts that inhabit a hogan where someone has died are called *chindis*. The dead person's name is not called out for fear the chindi might respond to the call. Most families still have medicine men who perform ceremonies to restore a

---

24. Greenberg, p. 73.
25. Ibid., p. 75.

sense of harmony, balance, beauty, and prosperity—the highest ideals of Navajo being, expressed by the concept of *hozjo*. Among the most common ceremonies still practiced are the *kinaalda*, a girl's puberty rite, and the *nidaa*, or squaw dance, a three-day ceremony performed in the summer.[26]

Today, on more than fifteen thousand square miles of mesa lands, some two hundred thousand Navajos live in widely scattered hogans, making their living raising sheep and cultivating crops.

APACHE

Throughout the Spanish period, the Apaches, like the Navajos, remained on the periphery of the Spanish administrative-missionary system. Their territory never became the setting of actual Spanish settlements. Notwithstanding, there was contact—first, through mutual raiding and active hostilities and second, through acquaintance with Spanish material culture. For example, the use of horses and better war equipment came from the Spaniards.[27]

The Apache believe in a supreme being called *Usen*, the giver of all life. Usen is of no sex or site and can be approached only through a medium; every Apache has his or her own medium that serves as a guardian spirit. The medicine man is a powerful influence among the Apache to this day. Many place more trust in the medicine man than in the Indian tribal leaders, whom many feel have been overly influenced by the white man and his institutions. Traditionally, the Apache practiced polygamy; the shortage of males in this warrior society made this necessary.

Today, at the beginning of the twenty-first century, there are two major Apache tribes living in New Mexico. The Mescalero Apaches live on a large reservation east of the Rio Grande between Alamogordo and Roswell in the south-central part of the state. Established in 1873, this reservation, with a population of about three thousand tribal members, is the site of several significant tribal business enterprises,

---

26. Ibid., p. 76.
27. Spicer, p. 241.

including Ski Apache, one of the largest ski resorts in the South-west, and the Inn of the Mountain Gods, a $20 million luxury resort complex opened in 1975. The Jicarilla Apaches live on an expansive reservation on the Continental Divide some ninety miles from Farm-ington in the north-central part of the state. Known for their business acumen, their main source of income is from sheep ranching, sub-stantially augmented by revenue from hundreds of gas and oil wells.

COMANCHE

The Comanche were true Plains Indians, with a range as wide as the buffalo's, from Nebraska and Kansas to the Llano Estacado of Texas and southeastern New Mexico. The Comanche were bitter enemies of the Apache and rarely ventured into Apache areas. When they did, it was generally on the way to raids in Mexico. In the 1780s, the Spaniards recruited some Comanche to help them fight the Apache. The raids of the combined forces were successful enough to allow a little breathing room for the Spanish occupiers. Little is known of the Comanche except that, in the words of historian T. R. Fehrenbach, "the Comanches conquered and controlled the plains for more than a hundred years, destroying the ancient dreams of Spanish empire in North America, blocking the French advance into the Southwest, and becoming, for more than sixty years, the single greatest obstacle to America's western expansion."[28]

---

28. Fehrenbach, *The Comanches: Destruction of a People.*

CHAPTER THREE

The Spaniards Arrive

New Mexico's second discoverers were soldiers. . . . With the soldiers came their men of religion. Franciscan friars walked in sandaled feet, meek and unarmed, but as determined as any soldier to conquer in the name of the cross they bore.

—Erna Fergusson, *New Mexico: A Pageant of Three Peoples*

Modern European expansion began in the fifteenth century and, over the next two centuries, proceeded to ensnare in its realm of influence the indigenous peoples of the Americas, Africa, southern Asia, and the islands of the South Seas. The Spaniards were the first to arrive in the Americas and, with surprising success, added a new Spain to their overseas empire. Within two generations of the landing of Christopher Columbus on a remote Caribbean island in 1492, Spaniards had conquered the Aztec Empire in Mexico and the Incas of Peru.

SPAIN'S EXPANSION INTO THE NEW WORLD

The successes of Hernando Cortés in Mexico and of Francisco Pizarro in Peru encouraged further exploration for other wealthy areas. Inspired by the many myths circulating at the time—a sea passage called the Strait of Anián, which allegedly led directly to the Indies; the Island of Pearls, where treasures were in abundance; and the fabled Seven Lost Cities of Antilla—expectations were high.[1]

---

1. Lavin, *Arizona: An Illustrated History,* p. 50.

The myth of Antilla, a variant of a tale long popular in Medieval Spain, was constantly on the Spaniards' minds when they arrived in the New World. The story told of seven bishops and their followers who fled Spain ahead of the Moorish invasion in the twelfth century. Sailing westward across the Ocean Sea (undoubtedly the Atlantic), they eventually landed on the island of Antilla. There, each bishop established a city that became fabulously wealthy: streets paved with gold, houses made of silver, and walls studded with rubies and emeralds. The earliest Spanish explorers fully expected to find Antilla, and their dreams of doing so were greatly enhanced by their stunning conquest of the Aztecs. As a result, the Spaniards were prepared to accept every ludicrous tale that reached their ears. Marc Simmons writes how they took particular notice of any reference to the magical number seven, with the persistent rumor of seven Indian towns in the jungles of western Mexico and the story of the seven caves spoken about in myths of both the Maya of Yucatan and the Aztecs.[2] It was no surprise that the 1536 tale about seven golden cities off to the north, which the Indians called Cibola, was inevitably associated with the mythical tale of Antilla.

Cabeza de Vaca's Adventures in Search of Cibola

The legend of Cibola first surfaced when four shipwrecked sailors, sole survivors of the failed Narváez Expedition that had sailed from Cuba in 1528 to colonize Florida, wandered into Culiacán, a community northwest of Mexico City, in 1536. Álvar Núñez Cabeza de Vaca and his companions—Castilla de Maldonado, Dorantes de Carranza, and Estéban the Moor (de Carranza's African slave)—told of their eight-year odyssey from Florida across Texas and New Mexico, then southward over the Chihuahuan Desert and the Sierra Madre Mountains to the northern frontier of *Nueva Galicia*. They talked of tales they occasionally heard from Indians along the way of "great cities" far to the north where the people lived in large homes with

2.   Simmons, *Interpretive History*, p. 14.

Álvar Núñez Cabeza de Vaca crossing the Great American Desert.
(ENGRAVING 1880)

gold-plated and turquoise-studded walls. As corroborative evidence, de Vaca presented five malachite arrowheads given to him by a band of Utes Indians. The stones' green color quickly transformed them into emeralds in the minds of Spaniards eager to believe that a "new" Mexico, a land of untapped wealth rivaling that of recently conquered Tenochtitlán, lay somewhere beyond the northern frontier. In an age when superstition prevailed over practical knowledge, it was not difficult to find support for the idea that Cibola might be the Seven Lost Cities of Antilla. As might be expected, the rumor spread like wildfire, sparking a renewed interest in the Spanish quest to find the "new" Mexico that had so far escaped them. His Excellency Don Antonio de Mendoza, viceroy of New Spain, was ecstatic when he heard the news that Cibola might be Antilla. A crafty man, his first move was to purchase the slave Estéban from his master, de Carranza (who was returning home to Spain), anticipating Estéban's usefulness in locating Cibola. de Mendoza then decided to send a small reconnaissance party, rather than a full-scale expedition, to explore the mysteries of the north country and to report back to him personally. Of course, the slave could not lead the expedition, so de Mendoza selected as leader Marcos de Niza, an audacious Franciscan friar who had been with Pizarro during the conquest of Peru, had a lot of frontier experience, and was skilled in celestial navigation and astronomy.[3]

Fray de Niza's Expedition in Search of Cibola

Fray de Niza set out from Mexico City, accompanied by his guide, Estéban the Moor, and a party of friendly Indians. When they reached Compostela in December 1538, the new governor of Nueva Galicia, Coronado, welcomed them. From Compostela, de Niza and his party followed familiar trading trails through the land of the Tepehuano and the Opata. One member of his party, Fray Onorato, fell sick at the Sinaloa River and had to be taken back to Culiacán. The others proceeded onward, fording the Fuerte River. Fray de Niza decided, upon reaching the Mayo (the next big river north of the Fuerte) to let

---

3.   Knaut, *The Pueblo Revolt of 1680,* pp. 21–23.

Estéban go on ahead with instructions to send back a messenger with a palm-high cross if he ran into anything important. In the meantime, de Niza crossed the Río Mayo and reached the Indian village of Vacapa, where he awaited news from Estéban. Four days after they had separated, a messenger bearing a large cross arrived with the announcement that Estéban was on his way to the Seven Lost Cities of Cibola, the first of which was only thirty days off.[4] It is believed that Estéban and his party trekked northward for many days to a Tepehuano village, where the four survivors of the shipwreck had previously stopped on their journey and had curiously named the place the "Town of Hearts." Estéban's party continued on for two more weeks, until they approached the outskirts of a cluster of pueblos belonging to the Zuni people, located just inside the boundary line of present-day New Mexico. They had found the fabled place of Cibola about which natives to the south had spoken in awe. Estéban forged ahead and entered the first Zuni pueblo, called Hawikuh. What happened when the party arrived is not clear, but it appears that Estéban ignored the Zunis' warning not to enter the village. The Zuni attacked, capturing and killing all but three of Estéban's party. According to some sources, Estéban's body was dismembered and pieces sent to each of the seven pueblos as proof that he was a mere mortal and as a way of dispersing any magic powers that he might possess.[5] The three members of the entourage who escaped made it back to de Niza with the tragic news. What happened next is a mystery. Some believe that after raising a cross and claiming the region in the name of the viceroy, de Niza and his remaining party hastily retraced their steps to Mexico City, where he gave a falsified explanation to the viceroy of what happened at Cibola. In his report, he gave dramatic details of Estéban's death (which he had not witnessed) and explained his own death-defying push to see Cibola for himself. He wrote:

> In the end, seeing that I was determined, two chiefs said that they would go with me (on to Hawikuh). With these and my

---

4. Beck, pp. 42–44.
5. There is a Zuni legend that tells of a "black Mexican with 'chili lips' who came from the 'land of everlasting summer' and was killed by their ancestors." (Lavin, p. 53)

own Indian interpreters, I pursued my journey until I came within sight of Cibola, which is situated in a plain at the base of a round hill. It has the appearance of a very beautiful city, the best I have seen in these parts. The houses are of a style the Indians have described to me, all made of stone, with their stories and terraces, as it appeared to me from a hill where I was able to view it. The city is larger than the city of Mexico. At times I was tempted to go to it, because I knew I risked only my life, which I had offered to God on the day I began this journey. But finally I realized, considering my danger, that if I died, I would not be able to make my report of this country, which to me appears the greatest and best of the discoveries. I commented to the chiefs who had accompanied me; and they told me it was the poorest of the seven cities, and the Totonteac (thought to be one of the Hopi villages) is much larger and better than all the seven, and that it has so many houses and citizens it has no end.

Under the circumstances, it seemed appropriate to me to call the country the new kingdom of Saint Francis; and there with the aid of the Indians, I made a great heap of stones, and on top of it placed a cross, small and light only because I had not the means of making it larger, and I declared that I erected that cross and monument in the name of Don Antonio de Mendoza, viceroy of New Spain, for the Emperor, our Lord, as a sign of possession, conforming to my instruction, and by which possession I proclaim that I took all of the seven cities and the kingdoms of Totonteac and of Acus and of Marata, and that the reason I did not go to these latter places was in order to give an account of all I did and saw.[6]

Researchers of New Spain's history have been baffled as to why de Niza wrote this inaccurate and absurd impression of his expedition. Conceivably, the mythical cities of gold, not to mention thousands of heathen souls, were out there waiting to be redeemed. Alex Shumatoff

---

6.   Lavin, pp. 54–55; also Shumatoff, *Legends of the American Desert.*

suggests that perhaps de Niza could not return empty-handed to the viceroy, or that the distinction between what was real and imagined was not always clear, particularly when traversing a desert awash with mirages.[7]

When Fray Marcos's story leaked out, all of Mexico City was abuzz. In no time, the embellished story included mention of abundant gold and other treasures and of civilized people who wore fine clothes and rode on exotic beasts. To keep the news from the ears of rival conquistadors in Cuba and Spain while he considered what to do, the viceroy banned everyone from leaving the colony without his permission. Clearly a full-scale military campaign was needed this time. Recruits for the expedition were not hard to find. Twenty years after Cortés's conquest of Mexico, the city was crawling with dashing young adventurers, spoiling for a chance to venture forth into the great unknown to conquer another Montezuma and his treasure for Spain.

Vásquez de Coronado's Expedition in Search of Cibola

Twenty-nine-year-old Francisco Vásquez de Coronado was awarded the honor of leading the campaign. His expedition, as were all such Spanish colonial enterprises of the time, was privately financed. Coronado's family invested fifty thousand ducats in the expedition, while Viceroy Mendoza personally put up an additional sixty thousand.

On February 22, 1540, Coronado set out from Compostela, the capital of Nueva Galicia, in search of Cibola. It was a magnificent display, with Coronado in gilded armor at the head of an expedition of three hundred Spanish soldiers armed with crossbows and arquebuses and protected by heavy leather jerkins and steel helmets. Three hundred Mexicans (as Mexican-born Spaniards were already called), a thousand Indian servants, extra horses, pack mules and cattle, and sheep for food accompanied them. They were given a splendid sendoff, led by the viceroy himself. The entourage stretched for miles as it proceeded northward along the west coast of Mexico. Much of

---

7.   Shumatoff.

the journey was more difficult than expected and required traversing miles and miles of scorched and uninhabited desert.[8] Entering what is present-day Arizona a few miles west of Bisbee, the Spaniards followed the San Pedro Valley and then headed eastward toward the Gila River, where they rested for several days. The convoy moved northward through the rugged White Mountains of eastern Arizona for another sixteen days. Finally, the exhausted party reached the outskirts of Hawikuh, the most western of the Zuni villages (near present-day Gallup in New Mexico), on July 7, 1540. It became evident as they drew near that de Niza's dazzling city perched on a plateau was nothing more than "mud-walled" villages. There were no roofs of gold and no treasure. Pedro de Castañeda, the group's chronicler, described their reaction to what they saw: "When they saw the first village, which was Cibola, such were the curses that some hurled at Friar Marcos that I pray God may protect him from them. It is a little, crowded village, looking as if it had been crumpled all up together."[9]

Smoke signals on a nearby hill alerted the Spaniards that their arrival had not passed unnoticed. A clash ensued when Zuni leaders sent word to Coronado that his presence was not welcome. This fight, which took place on July 7, 1540, is considered the first formal engagement between the European invaders and the Indians in what is today the continental United States. A footnote in history, it nonetheless marks the beginning of the clash of two cultures that would be repeated many times over the next several hundred years.

Zuni warriors made a formidable stand, but Coronado's well-disciplined cavalry prevailed, and the natives retreated to the sanctuary of their pueblos. Coronado then met with the Zuni headmen, exploring ways the two sides might coexist peacefully together. During the course of their meeting, the Zuni spoke of seven villages some twenty-five leagues west, where Tusayans lived on the high mesas. The Spaniards would later call these people the Moquis, known today as the Hopi.

Coronado sent out an exploratory party led by Pedro de Tovar to meet with the Hopis. De Tovar, with a party of seventeen horsemen,

---

8.   Fergusson, *Three Peoples*, p. 139.
9.   Lavin, p. 56.

Battle of Hawikuh—Coronado's attack on July 6, 1540. (DRAWING BY KENNETH CHAPMAN, 1915)

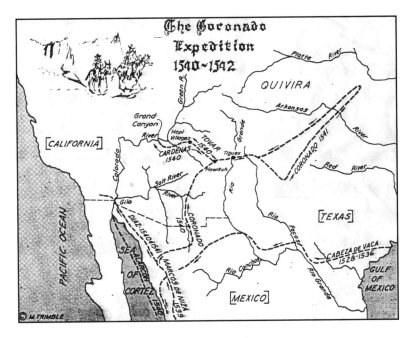

Map of Coronado Expedition, 1540-1542. (COURTESY OF MARSHALL TRIMBLE, DIRECTOR OF THE MARICOPA COMMUNITY COLLEGE SOUTHWEST STUDIES PROGRAM)

a few foot soldiers, and Franciscan missionary Father Juan Padilla (a veteran of Cortes's conquest of Mexico), marched to the eastern-most villages of the Hopis in what is now called the Jeddito Valley. At Kawaiokuh, de Tovar was received with hostility as the Hopis lined up for battle. De Tova, after some unproductive discussion with the Hopis through his Zuni interpreters, and with the sanction of the padre, discontinued further talks and attacked. The Hopis were quickly defeated and their village of Kawaiokuh was partly destroyed. The inhabitants then agreed to swear loyalty to the king of Spain. De Tovar stayed a few days, visiting all the villages before rejoining Coronado.[10] Another version of de Tovar's visit to Kawaiokuh describes how the Hopis had been waiting for the return of a long-lost white brother called Pahána. Pahána, the "One from Across the Water" or "Lost White Brother," was to return around the year 1520. When Pedro de Tovar arrived twenty years later in 1540, close to the predicted time for the Pahána's return, many Hopi elders believed that de Tovar was indeed Pahána, although they remained skeptical about whether this was the fulfillment of their prophesy. The legends prescribed very specific rituals and acts that would be performed by both the tribal elders and by the Pahána. At dawn the following morning the elders descended from the mesa, performed a ritual drawing of a line in the dust with corn, and approached Pahána (de Tovar), hands extended and palms up. The ritual reply of the true Pahána would have been to approach the elders with his hands extended and palms down. The reunion was to be completed by a grasping of the hands in a gesture of unity. Unhappily, the Hopis quickly discovered that de Tovar was not Pahána when the Spaniards charged the unarmed elders as they awaited the reciprocal gesture.

Discovering the Grand Canyon

Coronado, believing that the mighty river to the west could be the fabled Strait of Anián (the mythical passage to the Orient), sent García López de Cárdenas at the head of another expedition to investigate.

10. Spicer, p. 189.

Bill Ahrendt painting depicts García López de Cárdenas finding the Grand Canyon. (PHOTO BY GARY JOHNSON, COURTESY OF MARSHALL TRIMBLE, DIRECTOR OF THE MARICOPA COMMUNITY COLLEGE SOUTHWEST STUDIES PROGRAM)

After several days of exploring the high plateau, they came upon the spectacular Grand Canyon, its immense vertical walls jutting up like medieval cathedrals. From where they stood on the rim, they saw the river snaking its way through the gorge far, far below. Cárdenas and his men spent the next few days poised on the rim, gazing upon this geologic phenomenon and examining ways to get to the bottom. Three soldiers tried to descend the almost vertical wall, but they made it only part way before giving up.[11] When the discouraging news got back to Coronado, he decided against future quests to the west and turned his attention eastward toward the Rio Grande region.

EXPLORING THE RIO GRANDE AND PUEBLO INDIANS

Coronado and his men were still camped at Hawikuh when Zuni messengers came with news that a party of trading Indians had arrived in the village from the east. The leader, nicknamed Bigotes (meaning "Whiskers") by the Spaniards, went to see Coronado. During the parley that followed, Bigotes told Coronado of numerous pueblos along the banks of a river east of Hawikuh. Coronado seized on this intelligence and sent one of his lieutenants, Hernando Alvarado, and a handful of soldiers to explore the places described by Bigotes. They found twelve Tiwa (or Tigua) pueblos clustered in an area north of present-day Albuquerque. They found other villages north and south along a river they named Rio del Norte, known today as the Rio Grande. Among the villages they visited were Acoma, Tiguex, and Pecos. Like Hawikuh, the villages resembled multistoried apartments, with ladders or notched logs giving access to upper levels.[12]

When the exploring party returned, Alvarado described what they had seen. On Alvarado's advice, Coronado camped with his men at Tiguex (a pueblo near present-day Bernalillo) on the Rio Grande, where they spent the bitter-cold winter of 1540–1541. When Coronado and his men arrived, they forced the Tiwa to vacate one of their villages and let the soldiers have the quarters. This infuriated

---

11. Lavin, p. 58.
12. Ibid., p.59.

the Indians, but they had no choice. The soldiers then insisted that the Tiwas furnish them with food, clothing, and women. The Indians rebelled and Coronado's men retaliated by capturing two hundred Indians and executing them, burning them at the stake.[13] Wholesale fighting broke out, but it was soon brought under control by the superior Spanish soldiers. Two villages were destroyed and most of the Indians in them were killed. Coronado and his men (disappointed by their failure to find treasure) decided to leave Tiwas. By this time, the Spaniards were identified as ruthless plunderers.

QUIVIRA: CORONADO'S FINAL TREASURE HUNT

During their stay at Tiguex, the Spaniards met El Turco (The Turk), a Plains Indian, who captivated them with stories of a rich land to the east called Quivira, where gold and silver were in abundance. Coronado, greatly in need of a triumph of some kind, looked to Quivira to translate legend into reality. The onset of winter, however, prevented him from heading eastward. When spring arrived he formed an exploration party and, with guides, El Turco, and a Wichita Indian slave named Isopete, pushed eastward across the Texas panhandle and into present-day Kansas. They came to the end of their journey when they arrived at the grass houses of the Wichita Indians near present-day Lyons in central Kansas. This was El Turco's much bragged about Quivira. Under questioning by the Spaniards, the mendacious El Turco told Coronado that he had conceived the ploy to help New Mexico's Indians get rid of them. He was executed on the spot.[14]

Coronado and his men returned to the Rio Grande, having failed yet another time to find the mythical cities. On his return trip, he fell from his horse, was trampled by another horse, and sustained a serious head injury. Coronado was well enough to travel by the spring of 1542, so he and the remnants of his once impressive army set off for Mexico City. Two priests and several Indian servants from his party elected to stay behind and were never heard from again.

---

13. Spicer, p. 155.
14. Roberts, pp. 81–82.

After a brief stay in Mexico City, Coronado resumed his post as governor of Nueva Galicia. He was placed on trial in 1544, charged with mismanaging the expedition and with cruelty to the natives of the land he explored and convicted of "general neglect of duty . . . rank favoritism and numerous irregularities."[15] In time, the high court of New Spain overturned his conviction, but he was a broken man, having failed to find any new riches for Spain. His health gave way and he died in 1549.

Nueva Mexico

Coronado and his men could, however, point to a number of accomplishments in their 1540 expedition. They explored vast stretches of land north of New Spain and were the first Europeans to view the Grand Canyon and probe the interior of Puebloland. They claimed a Nueva Mexico for Spain. According to Spicer's account, in the northern fringes of New Spain the Spaniards came across a region frozen in time since the collapse of the Hohokam and the Anasazi cultures. There were some forty-five tribal groups throughout an area stretching from Pueblo, New Mexico, to the southern Sierra Madre— all of whom lived in small, autonomous, localized communities that were economically and politically independent of one another. They spoke twenty or more languages, similar enough to each other to show that they belonged to a single linguistic family. In these respects, these Indians presented a quite different set of problems to the Spaniards than did the Indians of central Mexico, where the existence of already developed dynasties made for easy conquest and cultural domination.[16]

---

15. Ibid., pp. 81–82.
16. Spicer, p. 153.

CHAPTER FOUR

Early Spanish Colonization Efforts

> When Coronado left Tiguex, three friars in his command had elected to stay on in that New Land; the wealth they sought was there in plenty: souls to be saved. But no word of them had come back from the mysterious north.
>
> —Erna Fergusson, *New Mexico: A Pageant of Three Peoples*

The region that would become *la Nueva Mexico* was all but forgotten for nearly forty years after Coronado returned home from his expedition beyond the northern frontiers of New Spain. It was not the failure of the Coronado venture alone that caused the Spaniards to turn their backs on the area; war with the Indians along the northern frontier prompted a more cautious approach toward establishing new settlements remote from populated communities.[1] There were other reasons as well: discovery of several spectacular silver deposits northwest of Mexico City beckoned large numbers of prospectors and miners, and settlers began farming and ranching in the areas surrounding the mines.

However, the Spaniards never lost interest in the lands still farther to the north, which they had begun referring to as Nueva Mexico. They continued to dream of finding the elusive seven cities of ancient legend or to discover an empire more splendid than Montezuma's or riches more abundant than the gold of the Incas. But riches and mythical legends were not the only inducements luring the Spaniards

---

1. Beck, p. 48 (citing Hubert E. Bolten, *The Spanish Borderlands*, p. 169).

northward. There was also strong missionary zeal—the determination to save the souls of the heathen Indians and the conviction that Catholic Spain was chosen for that mission. Historians write that the Spaniards' missionary zeal originated in the Middle Ages when they struggled to free their Iberian homeland from the Islamic faith of the Moors, and that their triumph over the Moors, as well as their discovery of the New World, inflamed their zeal.

Renewed interest in Nueva Mexico led to four expeditions in the last two decades of the sixteenth century. Agustín Rodríguez, a Franciscan lay brother, was given permission to undertake the first expedition into the territory in 1581, ostensibly to save the souls of the heathen Indians. He was saving souls among the Conchos Indians of southern Chihuahua when he heard reports of an advanced agriculture people who lived far to the north. After receiving permission from the viceroy, he put together an expedition consisting of two additional Franciscans, Fray Francisco López and Fray Juan de Santa María, nine soldiers led by Captain Francisco Chamuscado, and nineteen Indians. The party took off from Santa Barbara on the Mexican frontier on June 5, 1581. Instead of taking the same route as that of the first expedition led by Fray Marcos, they followed the Conchos River to the Rio Grande and followed it westward to El Paso. From El Paso, they traveled north until they reached the first Indian pueblo near what is now Socorro. From there, it is believed, they went north to Taos and on to the plains area beyond the Pecos River, before retracing their steps and heading westward to Acoma and Zuni.

The sole achievement of this expedition was the tracing of a new route. Hostile Indians killed Fray Juan de Santa María when he ventured off and separated himself from the others. When Captain Chamuscado decided to return to New Spain, Frays Rodríguez and López elected to stay behind and continue their missionary work among the Indians. The remainder of the expedition arrived home in April 1582 without Captain Chamuscado, who became ill and died along the way.

Concern for the safety of the Franciscans left behind led Fray Bernardino Beltrán to organize the next expedition. A wealthy rancher, Antonio de Espejo, agreed to finance and lead the trip. Some writers suggest that Espejo's reason for doing so was to escape punishment for having killed one of his ranch employees. The party set out in November 1582 with two friars, fifteen soldiers, and a few Indian servants, taking a route similar to that taken by Rodríguez and his party. At Puaray (the ruins are in Coronado State Monument near Bernalillo), they were told that the two priests they had come to rescue had been killed.[2] At that point, the two friars wanted to return home immediately, but Espejo managed to keep the group together and continued his exploration for gold and silver. It was the search for gold and silver, as some writers hint, that influenced his generosity in the first place. Overruling the objections of Fray Bernardino, Espejo took his party onto the tablelands west of the Rio Grande, where he cast a wider loop than had any Spaniard before him. Returning to the Rio Grande, he encountered hostility among the Indians at Puaray, and in retaliation he sacked the pueblo and executed sixteen captives. Espejo returned home in August of 1583, having been away nine months, during which time he had covered more than 3,500 miles. He wrote a grandiose account of his venture, greatly exaggerating the resources and population of the area. He addressed it to the king, hoping to obtain authorization to establish a colony there.[3] While his report attracted much interest back in Mexico City, his petition to colonize the area he called Nueva Mexico was left to others to accomplish.[4]

FIRST COLONIZING EXPEDITION OF NUEVA MEXICO

The belief that Sir Francis Drake had found a passage through Asia while on his homeward journey from his around-the-world voyage (1577–1580) influenced the Spaniards to begin colonizing the vast inland territory to the north of New Spain.[5] Because of this, the king signed a royal decree in Madrid on April 19, 1583, directing the viceroy to select a responsible subject who would, at his own expense,

2. Fugate and Fugate, p. 27.
3. Beck, p. 51.
4. Espejo was first to use the words *Nueva Mexico* in referring to the area we now know as New Mexico.
5. Beck, p. 52.

undertake settlement of the northern lands and the conversion of the native people.

The viceroy chose Don Juan de Oñate, son of silver baron Don Cristobál from the mining town of Zacatecas, to lead the first colonizing expedition. His family was wealthy, and he had many wealthy friends. While in his teens he had joined the military and spent many years fighting the Chichimeca Indians. He was married to Isabel Cortez Tolosa, daughter of a mine owner and descendent of Hernando Cortés. She died prematurely in the 1580s, and, according to friends, Juan was so overcome with grief that he turned his attention toward New Mexico as a place to escape his anguish. Oñate's contract required him to raise a force of two hundred men and provide them with all essential supplies to meet their needs for one year. In return for his investment in the expedition, Oñate would receive the title of governor, a salary of six thousand ducats a year, certain tax exemptions, the right to bestow the title of *Hidalgo* (member of the lower nobility) on his followers and the right to distribute land and Indian tribute to them as well. The royal treasury picked up the cost of five missionaries and a lay brother.

As preparations neared completion in the fall of 1595, a shift in viceroys followed by bureaucratic wrangling forced an almost three-year delay in the final authorization to proceed, running up Oñate's costs and endangering the project. In the interlude, two unauthorized expeditions entered New Mexico, but neither was successful. Gaspar Castaño de Sosa led one of them, proceeding with some 170 men, women, and children from Almadén along the Rio Grande to a spot near present-day Santo Domingo. There, in 1590, they briefly made a settlement before being ordered to abandon it and return to New Spain.

Castaño de Sosa had tried to colonize New Mexico, even though he had no direct grant from the king to do so. He did it by attempting to circumvent the Royal Ordinance of 1573 which restricted unauthorized settlements and redefined the concept of conquest, replacing it with a concept of pacification that provided for strict standards of conduct for colonists, soldiers, and the clergy in their dealing with the natives. He reasoned, incorrectly, that the ordinance applied only to "new discoveries" and not to New Mexico, which had already been discovered by Coronado and others.[6] His success was short-lived. A company of soldiers arrived in New Mexico in March 1591 with an order of arrest issued by the viceroy. De Sosa was placed in chains and returned to Mexico City, where he stood trial and was convicted of several charges, including that of trying to settle New Mexico without a direct grant from the king. As punishment, he had to leave the Americas.

Not long after the Castaño de Sosa episode, Captain Francisco Leyva de Bonilla, a Portuguese captain in the service of Spain, was dispatched by Governor Diego de Velasco of Nueva Vizcaya to track down a renegade band of Indians who were attacking cattle ranches along the Nueva Vizcayan frontier and into Nueva Mexico. Once across the border, de Bonilla and his party decided to explore New Mexico and the plains beyond, leading some historians to conclude that his trek was a pretense for pursuing the age-old dream of discovering the wealthy kingdom of Quivira. The venture carried de Bonilla and his party to the pueblo of San Ildefonso, above present-day Santa Fe, where they remained for most of a year, exploiting the local Pueblos. To rid themselves of their unwanted guests, the Pueblos retold the story of Quivira that had been told to Coronado some forty years earlier. Accepting the story as gospel, the de Bonilla party mounted their steeds and headed northeast via Cicuye (Pecos) onto the Great Plains. They finally arrived at the real Quivira, which turned out to be no more than an agricultural Indian village of grass huts on what was probably the Arkansas River near Wichita in present-day Kansas. After a few days rest, the expedition continued their journey for another twelve days until they reached a larger river, believed to have been the Platte, in what is now Nebraska. According to a Mexican Indian named Juseps, who was with the party, Captain de Bonilla was stabbed to death during a quarrel with his lieutenant, Antonio Guitérrez de Humaña, who then assumed command.[7]

Oñate's expedition finally took off on its journey to colonize New Mexico in January 1598. It consisted of 400 men, 130 wives and

---

6. Simmons, *Interpretive History*, pp. 32–33.
7. Source: www.tsha.utexas.edu/handbook/online/articles/print/BB/fbo16.html.

children, several Franciscan friars and lay brothers, and several hundred Indian servants. A large herd of livestock was driven along to provide meat, and oxen hauled the eighty-three carts carrying essentials.[8] The party followed the Conchos River before heading northward on a more direct route to the Rio Grande south of El Paso. It was there that Oñate formed an advance party of thirty soldiers and moved ahead of the main assemblage. Following the Rio Grande, he visited villages from Socorro northward. Stopping at each one, he told the natives, through his interpreters, that King Phillip of Spain owned all of the territory and that they must submit to his rule. He also told them that, in return, they would be protected from their enemies and be assured of God's kingdom in the hereafter.

A detailed account of the expedition was given by Gaspar Pérez de Villagrá, one of Oñate's lieutenants, in *Historia de la Nueva México,* published in Madrid in 1610. He wrote that the Indians were timid and fled at the sight of armored men on horseback but were lured back by trinkets. Villagrá was horrified at the paintings he saw in the kiva; *kachinas* (ancestral spirits) stared at him "like demons with fierce and terrible features." He reported seeing a more hideously shocking fresco at Tiguex: "Pictured upon the wall we saw the details of the martyrdom of those saintly men, Fray Agustín, Fray Juan and Fray Francisco. The paintings showed us exactly how they met their death, stoned and beaten by the savage Indians."[9]

Oñate, like his predecessors, followed the Rio Grande north. Swinging eastward to miss White Rock Canyon, he stopped at the Tewa village of Ohkay Owingeh, located in a fertile valley near the confluence of the Rio Grande and the Rio Chama. There Oñate established the first Spanish capital of New Mexico on July 11, 1598, and renamed the village San Juan de los Caballeros. Six months later, the Oñate party moved to the west side of the Rio Grande where they built the second capital and called it San Gabriel.

Oñate sent his lieutenants out from San Gabriel to explore his new realm. They fanned out over New Mexico in all directions, east to Picuris in the Santa Barbara Valley and over the divide to Taos and

---

8.   Fergusson, *Three Peoples,* p. 152.
9.   Ibid., p. 154.

Oñate Memorial near San Juan Pueblo, NM.

southwest, past San Marcos and Galistro, to Pecos. In a short time, Oñate and his lieutenants had covered much of the ground explored by Coronado and others before them. Like Coronado and others, they hoped to discover gold and spent much time searching for the wealth that was nowhere to be found. New Mexico was not Zacatecas. Many who accompanied Oñate on the expedition had done so in expectation of finding treasure, not to establish a colony in the wilderness. They had borrowed heavily from friends and relatives for the venture, and when they saw that the chances of success were not promising, they became embittered and disillusioned. Many attempts were made to desert and return to New Spain, and those who attempted to leave were dealt with harshly.

At the same time, the Franciscans began their task of "civilizing" the Pueblo Indians. They visited all the Tewa villages and built a *convento* in one and named it San Ildefonso. They established a mission at Santa Domingo and reported making converts among the Tiwa at Isleta and Sandia.[10] However, all was not tranquil with the Indians. Initially, they were cowed into obedience by their fear of the Spaniards. Later, as they became more self-assured, their fear gave way to expressions of defiance as the settlers consumed more than their share of the limited food supply. As their initial apprehension of the white man faded, some natives began to believe that, with their numbers, they could easily dispose of the handful of Spaniards in their midst.[11] It would soon lead to disaster for one pueblo.

NATIVES BATTLE SPANIARDS AT ACOMA

The Acoma Indians were the first of the Pueblo people to put the small Spanish enclave by the Rio Grande to its most severe test of survival. The event that led to this battle occurred on December 4, 1598, when a small Spanish party stopped at the Acoma pueblo to obtain food. They were part of Juan de Zaldivar's company of soldiers, making its way westward to join Oñate, who was on an exploratory trip to the

---

10. Ibid., p. 156.
11. Beck, p. 55.

sea. According to one version of the incident, the Indians lured the unsuspecting Spaniards up steep and narrow trails, supposedly to their provisions warehouse. The Indians ambushed them along the way; thirteen Spaniards were killed, including the commander, Juan de Zaldivar.[12] In the aftermath, fear gripped the colony. Worried over the loss of his limited supply of soldiers, Oñate appealed to the clergy and won their assurance that a retaliatory attack on Acoma would be justifiable. On January 12, 1599, Juan de Zaldivar's brother Vincente led the retaliation attack: "Seventy men, with weapons glinting in the winter sunlight, departed for Acoma like a medieval army bent on a crusade."[13]

After three days of fighting, the Spaniards had their victory, and hundreds of natives were killed and hundreds more taken prisoner. Those taken prisoner were put on trial. Oñate handed down cruel sentences. Warriors over age twenty-five had a hand or a foot cut off and were sentenced to twenty years in personal servitude; women over twelve were given twenty years of personal servitude and young girls were removed from their families and sent for the remainder of their lives to convents in Mexico City. The cruel punishments were doubtless intended as lessons to other natives who might be foolish enough to undertake similar attacks. It had its calculated effect, as it would be 1680 before Indians challenged Spanish rule again.[14]

MASS DESERTION OF SAN GABRIEL COLONISTS

While Oñate was dealing with the Acoma incident, discontent among the settlers had reached a point at which drastic measures were needed to control potential widespread desertions. Oñate ordered the slaying of one of his captains for stirring up unrest. When others attempted to leave, they were accused of treason and their leaders were executed.[15] These repressive actions only added to the existing unrest among the

---

12. Ibid., p. 56.
13. Simmons, *Interpretive History*, p. 40.
14. Beck, p. 57.
15. Ibid., p. 58.

struggling colonists. Oñate led a troop on an exploratory expedition eastward to Quivira in June 1601 in yet another unsuccessful attempt to find the wealth that had heretofore eluded him. During his absence, most of the colony deserted and made their way back to New Spain. On his return, Oñate found only some twenty-five Spaniards waiting to greet him. This sealed his fate. He was later tried and convicted for crimes committed during his term as governor, the most significant being the harsh measures he took against the Acoma Indians and the execution of members of his party who had attempted to leave the colony.

Colony Converted to Custodia and Juan de Oñate Removed

The desertion and news of the drastic measures used to control the New Mexico colony prompted a complete review of Oñate's project. The authorities in New Spain decided that the land lacked the great mineral wealth or significant agricultural potential to justify further expenditure and recommended that New Mexico be abandoned. The recommendation was forwarded to Madrid and was approved by the Crown. The decision, however, was never carried out; royal officials were at odds over what to do about the more than two thousand Christianized natives in the territory. It was royal policy not to abandon them, and it would be impractical to move them to New Spain. Finally, Madrid ruled in favor of turning the colony over to the Crown as a *custodia*, or mission station, with control in the hands of the clergy, and the military present only to protect the missionaries.

Spain's first attempt to colonize New Mexico had failed. In spite of his dedicated effort, Juan de Oñate's term as the first governor produced few achievements and many problems. He used his power unwisely, and for this he was punished. The Crown removed him from office in 1607. His sole contribution to New Mexico was serving as its first governor.

For sixteenth-century Spaniards, New Mexico had not produced the wealth they sought. Their dreams of finding the seven cities of ancient legend, or an empire more splendid than Montezuma's, were not realized. In the seventeenth century, however, the imagination of explorers and missionaries would be rekindled with new dreams of recolonizing New Mexico and of converting the natives to Christianity.

CHAPTER FIVE

Rise and Fall of the Great Missionary Era

The real story of the history of New Mexico in the seventeenth century is that of the bitter, and sometimes violent, conflict between church and state for supremacy.

—Warren A. Beck, *New Mexico: A History of Four Centuries*

Spain's interest in New Mexico began to wane once it was recognized that it contained neither great mineral resources nor significant agricultural potential. Governor Oñate was removed from office in 1607 and, the following year, King Phillip III issued an order to vacate the province and withdraw all the settlers. Before the king's order reached Mexico City, the viceroy of New Spain had sent two Franciscans, Fray Lazaro Ximenez and Fray Isidro Ordóñez, northward to investigate and report on the state of affairs in the northern colony. As might be expected, they wrote a highly favorable report, stating that the Indians were responding remarkably well and that there were many converts to the Christian faith. The findings were turned over to a committee of ecclesiastics who naturally recommended that the province not be abandoned, as it would be sacrilegious to surrender the converts to paganism. Bowing to the committee's recommendation, the king remanded his order and decided in favor of continuing the colony as a missionary province under royal patronage. The governor would be appointed either by the king or by the viceroy of New Spain, Franciscan friars would oversee the spiritual and welfare needs of the natives, and the military would serve essentially to provide protection.[1] All provincial officials, including the friars, would be compensated from the royal treasury.

Don Pedro de Peralta: The First Royal Governor

The first royal governor, Don Pedro de Peralta, arrived as a replacement for Governor Oñate in 1609. He brought instructions with him to move the province's capital and the colonists from San Gabriel to a more central location. It was believed that San Gabriel was too exposed and vulnerable in the event of Indian attacks. Construction commenced on the new capital in 1610 over the ruins of an abandoned Tanoan Indian village located in the foothills of a chain of mountains that would later be called *Sangre de Cristo* (Blood of Christ). The governor called his new capital Villa Real de la Santa Fe (Royal City of the Holy Faith).[2]

The tiny village of Santa Fe was connected with the outside world by a trading interchange known as the "mission supply service." Organized first in 1609 and reorganized in 1664, this service was meant to provide only for the missions in New Mexico. However, in actual practice, it became the commercial umbilical cord that connected the northern colony with Mexico City throughout much of the seventeenth century.

Conductas (caravans) consisting of upward of thirty-two wagons (each pulled by a team of eight mules and capable of carrying two tons of supplies) intermittently traveled the 1,500-mile route between Mexico City and Santa Fe. The journey, across deserts and mountain canyons and through Zacatecas and Durango, took from five to six months each way. On the northbound trip, the freight consisted largely of mission and church supplies—essential materials for the altar and clothing for the missionaries—but contained items of luxury

---

1. Fergusson, *Three Peoples,* p. 165.
2. Santa Fe's Palace of the Governors, completed in 1612, has the distinction of being the oldest government building in the United States.

goods as well.[3] On the return trip to Mexico City, the cargo consisted mostly of staple goods—hides, pine nuts, blankets, and so on. Warren A. Beck writes that, later in the century, flocks of sheep raised at the missions were driven with the caravans southward to be sold to the miners of New Spain, and Indian slaves were driven along with the flocks, also to be sold to the miners as slaves.[4]

Throughout most of the seventeenth century, the mission supply caravan was Santa Fe's vital link to New Spain and the civilized world beyond. Settlers, friars, public servants, and a host of others accompanied the caravan on their treks to and from the northern frontier. Many believe it was indispensable to the development of New Mexico; without it, the northern province might well have been abandoned altogether by Spain.

THE GREAT MISSIONARY ERA

It was at Santa Fe in 1610 that Governor Pedro de Peralta and Fray Isidro Ordóñez began the renewed colonization and conversion program of the Pueblo Indians that would last for over seventy years. During this period of New Mexico history, appropriately named the "Great Missionary Era," the Franciscan friars played the primary role in bringing Christianity and Spanish culture to the upper Rio Grande. They created their own private realm that operated practically independently of New Mexico's civil government through their network of missions stretching from Pecos on the edge of the plains to the western villages of the Hopi. They had their own ecclesiastical capital at Santo Domingo pueblo, a dozen leagues south of Santa Fe, where the head of the Order for New Mexico had his residence. He was a man of sufficient power and prestige to challenge, when he thought necessary, the authority of the governor.[5]

The friars were men of faith and courage dedicated to carrying the Christian faith to the natives of New Mexico. They set out at once

---

3. Fergusson, *Three Peoples,* p. 27.
4. Beck, p. 63.
5. Simmons, *Interpretive History,* p. 57.

to reinvigorate the Indians' declining Christianity, rebuild churches, and found new missions. They knew enough Indian words to explain basic doctrine and describe the sacraments. They attended the sick and gave comfort to the dying. They toiled day in and day out, fasted and prayed.

Churches were built in all the pueblos in the twenty year period after 1610, during which time secular and clerical leaders were chosen and installed in all the villages. The Indians were generally peaceful, and increasing numbers accepted the mission way of life. During this period the number of friars servicing the missions and schools continued to grow. Each mission was responsible for its dependent Indians and had its adjoining rancho, classrooms, and workshops where instruction was provided in subjects such as catechism, Spanish customs, carpentry, weaving, and the planting and harvesting of new crops, as well as many others.[6]

Friar Alonzo de Benavides, who arrived in 1625 and served as custodian of the colony for four years, delivered a report to the king of Spain in 1630, praising the success of the missionary work. Friar Benavides had special mention for a school "of all the arts" operating at Picuris. He spoke of "a marvelous choir of wonderful boy musicians" at Taos. He found "all baptized and well instructed" at Pecos. Even in rebellious Zuni, he was pleased that some boys had been taught to chant. Yet, he was disturbed that the Zuni "kept their sacred fires glowing." He also wrote of some troublesome goings-on; the Jemez, like the Zuni, were "indomitable and belligerent, above all, great idolaters."[7]

To many writers, Friar Benavides's glowing picture of peaceful natives and spiritual success on the Rio Grande was basically an appeal for additional funds and resources for the missions. At the time, the Indians were becoming increasingly, although passively, hostile and discontented in their relationship with the missionaries. Benavides did not mention this. Neither did he mention the bad example set by many Spaniards that was impeding the conversion of the natives

---

6.   Ibid., p. 58.
7.   Fergusson, *Three Peoples*, p. 173 (from "The Memorial of Fray Alonso de Benavides," translated by Mrs. Edward E. Ayer).

Mission San José, Luguna Pueblo.

Mission San Estevan, Ácoma Pueblo. (PHOTO BY LEON CANTRELL, 1948).

Church of St. Francis of Assisi at Ranches de Taos, built during the 1770s.
(PHOTO BY CLAIRE MATHER)

to Christianity. To the Indians, the word *Christian* had become synonymous with someone who came to kill and plunder them or sell them into slavery. Some Indians welcomed the priests, but they did not want Christians to come with them. There was a decline, rather than an advancement, in the extension of the mission system during the next fifty years. As elsewhere on the Spanish frontier, the underlying problem stemmed from the relations between the church and the civil authorities.[8]

CONFLICT BETWEEN CHURCH AND STATE

Seventeenth-century New Mexico experienced a bitter and sometimes violent conflict between the church and state for supremacy. This conflict was part and parcel of a larger struggle that extended to all of colonial Spanish America. It manifested most in New Mexico, however, for two reasons: the province's isolation made Spanish laws regarding the treatment of the natives difficult to enforce, and competition was fierce for Indian labor, virtually the only source of wealth in the poverty-stricken land.[9]

The quarrel between church and state began in the administration of Governor Peralta in 1612 and grew in intensity until it verged on civil war by 1650. While the conflict continued after that date, the intensity diminished somewhat. Over the years, the viciousness varied greatly, depending on the personalities of the governor and the friar in charge. Governor Peralta, whose administration began in 1609, was an able and tolerant administrator until he came face-to-face with Friar Ordóñez, who arrived to take charge of the missions in 1612. An arrogant and intolerant man, Ordóñez was convinced that all civil authority should be subordinate to him, and he took every opportunity to interfere with the civil functions of the governor. On one occasion, he intercepted troops on the road to Taos and ordered them back to Santa Fe to celebrate Pentecost. When the governor rescinded

8. Ibid., p. 152.
9. Beck, p. 64.

the order, Ordóñez excommunicated him and for penance ordered him to appear barefoot outside the church in Santa Fe.

Declaring himself an agent of the Holy Office, Ordóñez next threatened to excommunicate anyone who even spoke to the governor. When the governor decided to report Ordóñez to the viceroy in Mexico City, the good friar, invoking the authority of the Holy Office, had him arrested. On another occasion, Ordóñez asked for an escort to Mexico City to consult with his superiors about Peralta's behavior. When the governor informed him that he himself would be the escort, Ordóñez became so infuriated that he removed the governor's chair from its honored place near the altar in the church and placed it outside where the Indians sat. There, among the Indians, the humbled governor was forced to listen to the friar's invective preaching: "Let no one persuade you that I do not have the same power and authority that the Pope in Rome has. . . . I can punish any person who is not obedient to the commandments of the Church and mine."[10] But Ordóñez was not, as he claimed, an agent of the Holy Office. The many bitter accusations the friar sent to his superiors in Mexico City led to the replacement of both Ordóñez and Peralta. Ordóñez and Peralta were two powerful antagonists whose hostile behavior set the tone for church and state relations along the Rio Grande for another fifty years.

Conditions did not improve with the appointment of Juan de Eulate as governor in 1618. He was notorious for his tactlessness and his irreverence. He was contemptuous not only of the clergy but of everything about the church. He abused and insulted the friars and refused to encourage their missionary efforts. However, these were charges made against him by the friars, and historians question whether, in fact, he was as blameworthy as depicted. Like his predecessors, he looked on his appointment as a reward for previous services and an opportunity for personal gain.

The next governor, Felipe Sotelo Ossorio, took office in 1625. His appointment ushered in a brief truce between the executive branch and the clergy. Many attribute the calm to the new clerical leader, Friar Alonzo de Benavides, who arrived about the same time. Governor Sotelo was an able administrator who was very supportive of the mission work.

---

10. Ibid., pp. 172–173.

There followed a series of governors, most of whom were accused of forcing the Indians to work for them and of engaging in illegal trade. From 1637 to 1641, a long, drawn-out squabble between Governor Luis de Rosas and the friars brought church and civic relations into serious breach. During this time, Taos Indians killed their missionary and destroyed the church; the missionary at Jemez was also killed.[11] The usual charges and countercharges made their way southward to Mexico City, and, in the spring of 1641, Governor Rosas and the friar in charge were removed from office. But this was not the end of Rosas's problems. His enemies accused him of having an affair with the wife of an individual named Ortíz, leading to Rosas's assassination. A new governor, Alonso Pacheco, arrived in Santa Fe in the fall of 1642 and proceeded to conduct an investigation into his predecessor's murder. Eight soldiers, the ringleaders, were executed for their part in the assassination scheme.

The strife between missionaries and civic leaders continued unabated throughout the remainder of the 1640s and well into the 1650s. Peace reigned for a short while in the late 1650s, but only because the governor and the *custodio* (director of the Franciscan missionaries) were brothers. However, the conflict was renewed in 1659 when the new governor, Bernardo López de Mendizábal, and the new head of the Franciscans, Friar Juan Ramirez, were appointed. Both arrived in Santa Fe on the same supply caravan, where, it is said, their squabbling over authority immediately ensued en route. The new governor was not long in office before the usual accusations were brought against him. Most serious, however, were the charges of heresy brought against him and his wife, Doña Teresa. Nosy servants testified that they had been seen at night in their bedroom "performing acts that were sure proof of Judaism."[12] Both had been observed bathing and washing their hair on Friday nights, which, apparently, only Jews were permitted to do. Doña Teresa was also charged with reading a foreign language book, even laughing as she read. Both were eventually cleared of the charges against them, but the governor died before the Holy Office could complete its investigation.

---

11. Spicer, p. 158.
12. Beck, p. 175.

Don Diego de Peñalosa, the next governor, served from 1661 to 1664. His administration brought little improvement in relations with the clergy. A real breach came when he arrested the custodian, Friar Posada, who was also the Inquisitor for the province. Later, de Peñalosa was convicted by the Inquisition, sentenced to do penance in Mexico City, and was then banished from New Spain. He sought reprisal by going to the English and offering them a scheme to capture New Mexico. When that was unsuccessful, he went to France and met with King Louis XIV. However, the French showed little interest in his scheme, although some historians believe his conversations might have influenced the explorations later undertaken by La Salle.

LAND GRANTS: ALSO A SOURCE OF DISCORD

Another source of conflict that impeded relations between the two arms of New Mexico's colonial government was a land-grant system that was introduced as part of the colonization program undertaken by Don Juan de Oñate in 1598. To encourage colonization, grants of land were made to soldiers who participated in the conquest. These grants, or *encomiendas*, carried with them the right of *repartimiento* that is, the right to employ Indians living on the grants. The fruits of Indian labor went in part to the king and in part to the *encomenderos*, who were not permitted by law to reside on the property that they held as encomiendas. However, in New Mexico this law was largely ignored, causing unrelenting discord between the Spaniards who lived on their grants and the Indians. This conflict expressed itself in a variety of ways; civil authorities accused the missionaries of arbitrary and unjust treatment of Indians, and the missionaries, in turn, charged and, in many instances, produced confirming evidence that governors and their aides had not only physically abused Indians, but had also been guilty of setting bad examples by their own sexual misconduct and immoral behavior.[13]

---

13. Spicer, pp. 159–160.

HOLY OFFICE OF THE INQUISITION

There were other sources of conflict in the colony, the most serious arising from the Franciscans' attempt to stamp out Indian religious practices by forcible means. In the early years of the mission period, success in winning over the Pueblos had been accomplished through constructive mission work, such as building churches, caring for the sick, and introducing new agricultural crops and techniques. Although the Indians had accepted baptism and were more or less regular participants in church devotions, it was becoming apparent to the missionaries that they had not given up their old religious ways. The masked kachina dances were still performed, ceremonies in the village kivas were held, prayer sticks were offered, and corn-meal was still strewn ritually. Native affinity to the old ways seemed almost as strong as ever. While, at times, missionaries had taken steps to suppress Indian ceremonials, there had been a measure of tolera-tion until 1661, when the Franciscan custodian decreed an absolute prohibition of all kachina dances. Missionaries were instructed to seek out all materials of "idolatry," and kivas—the Pueblo ceremonial rooms—were raided. In a short time, hundreds of kachina masks, prayer feathers, and images of various kinds were confiscated and destroyed.[14]

THE GATHERING STORM

Spanish suppression of Pueblo religious practices and a persistent mistreatment of Indian labor reached a critical point in the 1670s. With their crops devastated by a continuous drought and beleaguered by ever-increasing Apache raids, the Pueblos placed the blame for their plight on the Spanish disruption of their religious practices. At the same time, famine and Apache raids were functioning to some extent to heal the decades-old church/state breach and bring church and state officials together on a somewhat more cooperative basis than at any time since the founding of the colony.

---

14. Ibid., p. 161.

In 1675, Governor Juan Francisco de Treviño cooperated with the missionaries in their efforts to combat growing Indian interest in reviving their sacred religious ceremonies by rounding up forty-seven Indian *caciques* (religious leaders) from various villages. They were accused, tried, and convicted of witchcraft, idolatry, or the promotion of idolatry. Four of the leaders were hanged; the others were severely flogged, admonished, and later released. Historian Spicer writes that it was the flogging of the caciques that provoked the great Pueblo Revolt of 1680, a rebellion more extensive that any previous uprising and with more serious consequences for the spread of Spanish civilization on the northern frontier.[15]

Among those flogged and released by the Spaniards was Popé, a Tewa-speaking Indian and powerful shaman from the village of San Juan. After his release, he sought refuge among the Tiwas of Taos, where he and other Pueblo leaders worked secretly on a plan to drive the Spaniards out of New Mexico once and for all. Their task could only be described as "against all odds." Not only did they have to overcome the villagers' natural aversion toward confederation, they had to contend with a minority of Indians who were still loyal to the Spaniards and who might betray the plot at any time.[16]

From his distant mountain kiva, Popé dispatched runners, sworn to secrecy under pain of death, to bring his message of liberation to every Pueblo in the Rio Grande valley. Slowly, a network of Pueblo leaders supportive of Popé's cause evolved. They included a host of war chiefs, their warriors, and, significantly, several prominent *mestizos* (person of mixed ancestry) and other persons of mixed heritage from more than two dozen Indian settlements, separated by hundreds of miles and six different languages. Popé chose August 12, 1680, as the date on which the revolt would take place. Three days before, he had dispatched runners, each carrying a cord of knotted maguey fiber with the knots signifying the number of days before the rebellion. "The cord was passed through all the pueblos of the kingdom so that the ones which agreed to it [the rebellion] might untie one knot in sign of obedience, and by the other knots they would know the

---

15. Ibid., p. 162.
16. Simmons, *Interpretive History,* p. 69.

days which were lacking; and this was to be done on pain of death to those who refused to agree with it."[17] Only the Piro Pueblos to the south—suspected as being untrustworthy—were excluded from the call to action. The inevitable happened on August 9, when the leaders of San Marcos, San Cristóbal, and La Ciénega opted out of the rebellion and informed Governor Antonio de Otermín of the impending revolt. Almost at the same time, messages reached Otermín from two Franciscan friars and the *alcalde* (local official) of Taos, confirming the rumors of a planned uprising. As reports of uprisings elsewhere continued to pour in, Otermín recognized the danger that now confronted every Hispanic colonist in New Mexico. Isolated in the distant northern colony, amid a Pueblo Indian population numbering close to seventeen thousand, the several hundred settlers, soldiers, and Franciscan missionaries in the region faced extinction should the rebellion be allowed to gather momentum.[18]

FALL OF THE SPANISH KINGDOM

On Saturday morning, August 10, 1680, the Pueblo Indians brought their remote corner of the Spanish Empire to its knees when they rose up in an awesome challenge against their Hispanic masters. That day, and those that followed, witnessed a massacre of colonists beyond description. Warrior bands rampaged across the countryside, attacking isolated farms and haciendas, killing entire families and wiping out community populations en masse. In the churches, priests were slain at their altars. Once the outlying districts had been thoroughly pillaged, the rebel Indians came together in a body and moved against the capital of Santa Fe itself.

The Indians surrounded Santa Fe on August 15, setting fire to the outskirts and the Church of San Miguel. Governor Otermín countered the advance with his entire force—fewer than one hundred men. The battle lasted most of the day, with many casualties on both sides. As darkness fell, Otermín and his troops withdrew to the palace. This

---

17. Knaut, p. 169 (citing from Declaration of Pedro Naranjo of the Queres Nation, December 19, 1680, Revolt 2:8) (The Pueblo Revolt of 1680).
18. Ibid., p. 7.

allowed the Indians to gain a position behind the *casas reales* (royal houses), from which they could fire into the plaza of the governor's home. At this point, the Indians cut the water supply, and an impasse followed that lasted until August 18. Desperate from thirst that had lasted two days and a night, Otermín concluded that "it would be a better and safer step to die fighting than of hunger and thirst, shut up within the casas reales (royal houses)."[19]

On the morning of August 20, the governor and all the troops he could muster charged forth from the palace and attacked the Indians. Before the hostilities ended at noon, three hundred Indians had been killed and forty-seven captured. Additionally, five Spaniards lay dead and many were wounded, including Governor Otermín. When the dust settled, Otermín briefly interrogated the forty-seven prisoners before summarily executing them under the charge of treason.[20]

SPANIARDS EVACUATE SANTA FE

The following day, Otermín hurried preparations to evacuate the capital and retreat south. He deemed it imperative to leave Santa Fe before the Indians recovered from their defeat and attacked again, and before persistent rumors of the impending arrival of Apache reinforcements proved true.[21] Along the escape route, signs of revolt were everywhere; abandoned pueblos, desecrated churches, religious images, and the bodies of those who were killed stood as gruesome reminders of the catastrophe that had taken place. The refugees reached La Salineta, just north of El Paso del Norte, on September 19; they numbered fewer than two thousand. Most were Indian servants, many of them inhabitants of the Piro pueblos in the southern reaches of the province who could not be relied on and had been excluded from the general rebellion by Popé.[22]

---

19. Ibid., p. 11.
20. Ibid.
21. Ibid.
22. Ibid., p. 14.

It has been estimated that 380 settlers were killed in the uprising and that twenty-one of the province's forty Franciscan friars had died, victims of their Pueblo parishioners. For the surviving refugees, it was the final chapter of the eighty-year Spanish presence in New Mexico. The revolt not only destroyed the New Mexico colony, but it also jolted the entire northern frontier of the viceroyalty and sent shock waves rippling through Mexico City and Madrid.

Governor Otermín and the refugees spent the winter that followed their exile from New Mexico at what was supposed to be a transitory camp near El Paso de Norte. The area was then under the jurisdiction of Nueva Vizcaya, but the viceroy gave Otermín authority to rule as if he were still in Santa Fe so that he could hold his people together with an exile government until it was time for an early reconquest of the rebellious province. In November, Otermín undertook such an attempt. He headed north to Isleta (the southernmost pueblo still occupied) at the head of a small army of fewer than 150 troops and Indian allies. He met no resistance at Isleta, but further north the Indians fled to the mountains as he and his men approached. As he continued, it became evident to him that the Indians were still extremely unfriendly. This unfriendliness, together with the raw winter weather and the shortage of forage for his horses, prompted him to withdraw to El Paso. The retaking of New Mexico would have to wait for another day. In the meantime, residents of the pueblos, for their part, had accomplished what no other American Indian tribe had hitherto achieved, and what none would achieve thereafter—a successful challenge to European domination in the New World.

CHAPTER SIX

Reconquest of New Mexico

The undertaking was viewed emotionally as another *reconquista*, paralleling, though on a smaller scale, Spain's recapture of territory from the infidel Moors during the Middle Ages.

—Marc Simmons: *New Mexico: An Interpretative History*

It took thirteen years for the Spaniards to take back New Mexico. The distinction of retaking the lost province belongs to Don Diego de Vargas[1] who is acclaimed as its El Reconquistador (The Reconqueror). He was born in Madrid of an illustrious Spanish family distinguished by generations of service to both church and Crown. Historians characterize him as having been an exceptional soldier, a proven administrator, a deeply religious man, and a man rich enough to reconquer the lost province "at his own expense."[2] In his dealings with the New Mexico natives, he was at one and the same time a courtly diplomat, a decisive military leader, and a resourceful campaigner.[3] Unfortunately, Vargas was capable of unyielding cruelty toward the Indians, a characteristic that was to prove costly to the Spaniards in the long run. However, historians believe that he deserves to be ranked with Coronado as one of the most important Spaniards in the history of New Mexico.

Vargas was appointed governor and captain-general of New Mexico in 1690, arriving at El Paso del Norte to assume his duties on February

---

1. Better known as Don Diego de Vargas Zapata y Luján Ponce de Leon y Contreras, he served two terms as governor general before dying in Bernalillo in 1704. His remains were later removed to the parish church in Santa Fe that was rebuilt into the cathedral, where they still lie.
2. Fergusson, *Three Peoples,* p. 181.
3. Beck, p. 84.

Don Diego de Vargas, Governor of New Mexico, 1691–97, 1703–04.

22, 1691. He found the exiled colony at San Lorenzo near present-day El Paso in deplorable condition—crop failures, continual raids by hostile Indians, and fading hopes for returning to their former homes in New Mexico had taken a toll on the group. Further, those who were eager to reclaim their former lands to the north lacked sufficient funds and equipment to prepare for the expedition. Nevertheless, the settlement had survived, and it would go on to provide the basis for the recolonization of Spanish New Mexico.

Eager to get on with the difficult assignment, Vargas set out from El Paso on August 21, 1692, at the head of a small force of sixty soldiers; he was accompanied by three friars and one hundred Indians. His strategy was to use his small force with maximum effectiveness; upon reaching the first pueblo, he would lay siege and prevent any of the inhabitants from escaping. He would then have everyone sing praises to the Blessed Virgin.[4] Next, the missionaries would try to persuade the Indians to return to the Catholic faith and submit to the Spanish Crown. Should the Indians accept, the friars would absolve all sins and baptize the children who had been born since the revolt of 1680. Vargas believed that if this strategy worked at the first pueblo, others would quickly follow suit and the conquest would be a swift and bloodless event. However, if there was resistance, Vargas was prepared to attack the besieged pueblo and use whatever force was necessary to obtain submission.

On the night of September 12, 1692, Vargas camped within sight of Villa Real, which was occupied by Tanos Indians. At dawn, he crossed the Santa Fe River at Agua Fria and approached the town from the northwest. He sent in one of his messengers with an offer of peace and pardon to all who would surrender. His masterful mix of diplomacy and the not-so-subtle threat of a siege worked; the Indians of Villa Real surrendered.[5] Vargas then set out for the northern pueblos. Luis Tapatu, pueblo leader at San Juan, appealed to Vargas for help against the raiding Apaches. Vargas offered him peace, forgiveness, and protection and rode on to his next stop, Santa Fe. There, he found the old Spanish capital fortified and its inhabitants less friendly.

---

4. Ibid., p. 85.
5. Fergusson, *Three Peoples*, pp. 181–182.

After lengthy and involved negotiations that could easily have erupted into hostilities with disastrous results for the Spaniards, Vargas finally convinced the Indians that it would be wiser for them to accept his terms than do battle. With similar offerings, he won over all the villages—Taos, Pecos, Jemez, Zuni, and distant Moqui (Hopiland). On his return from the west, Vargas left his inscription on El Morro: "Here was General Don Diego de Vargas who conquered for our Holy Faith and the royal crown all New Mexico at his own expense in the year 1692."[6]

The initial success of Vargas's bold campaign was, in many respects, due to circumstances among the Indians themselves. For example, the spirit of cooperation, displayed by the Indians during the revolt of 1680, had ceased to exist once the Spaniards, the common foe, were no longer mastering them. Further, the Pueblo Indians had splintered into many factions by 1692, and it was not unusual for these factions to be at war with one another. Governor Vargas knew he must recapture most of the province before the Pueblos could again unite.[7] In a vigorous four-month campaign, he had managed to restore twenty-three pueblos to Spain's empire and to the Christian faith, and he did it without firing a single shot or unsheathing a sword. Proclaiming a formal act of possession on September 14, 1692, Vargas was extolled as El Reconquistador of New Mexico.

SPANIARDS RETURN TO NEW MEXICO

Having obtained at least the tacit submission of the Pueblo Indians, Governor Vargas returned to El Paso to prepare for the actual resettling of the province. After months of preparation, he headed north again with eight hundred colonists, a large number of livestock, and the necessary supplies. When the caravan reached the upper Rio Grande area, friendly Indians warned Vargas to expect resistance from hostile Indians. The governor arrived at Santa Fe on December 16,

---

6.   Ibid., pp. 182–183.
7.   Bancroft, *History of Arizona and New Mexico 1530–1888*, pp. 184–186 (citing Jack D. Forbes, *Apache, Navaho, and Spaniard*, pp. 237–238).

1693, but he and his party were denied entry to the villa. He spent two unsuccessful weeks negotiating with the Indians to relinquish their claim to the capital. Finally, the governor moved to take Santa Fe by force, which was accomplished after a fierce battle that lasted two days. Thereafter, seventy Pueblo defenders were executed and several hundred captured men, women, and children were committed to slavery. The peaceful reconquest that Governor Vargas had anticipated had turned bloody.

While many of the Pueblos honored the pledges of submission they had made to Vargas in 1692, others recanted. The Tanos, who had settled farther north among the Tewa villages, did not surrender. Instead, they joined with San Ildefonso, the most defiant of the Tewa villages, in holding out against the Spaniards. From their stronghold on top of the Black Mesa, the Tanos, San Ildefonsans, and other Tewas joined in a nine-month resistance during 1694. They raided Santa Fe and harassed the resettled colonists from their headquarters.[8]

Governor Vargas managed to install a new administration in Santa Fe by late 1694. He commissioned a new villa to be built in Santa Cruz, thereby forcing the Tanos to relocate to the east near present-day Chimayo. Missionaries had started taking up residence in surrounding pueblos, and it appeared that the Spaniards were again well established. Nevertheless, a new revolt broke out in 1696. The Jemez people killed their missionary and, supported by warriors from Acoma and Zuni, stepped up an aggressive campaign against the colonists. Eventually, the Jemez were driven into the mountains, and many joined with the Navajos or went westward to live with the Hopis. After the Jemez rebellion was put down in 1696, a new, more widespread outbreak occurred. This time the hostilities came from the displaced Tanos at Chimayo, who were joined by the northern Tiwa of Taos, the Picuris, the Santo Domingans, and the Cochitis, while the Zia, Santa Ana, and San Felipe Pueblos remained loyal and fought with the Spaniards. Six missionaries and twenty-one other Spaniards were killed during these hostilities. The Spaniards eventually defeated or routed all the belligerents, and, after 1696, there were no further uprisings, and the Spanish colony began to take on a more permanent

---

8.   Spicer, p. 164.

appearance.[9] The initial party that had accompanied Governor Vargas from El Paso was augmented by the arrival of subsequent settlers and the colony grew with estancias and haciendas again appearing along the upper tributaries of the Rio Grande.

Post-Reconquest Era

The period from 1700 to the arrival of the Anglo-Americans in the 1840s was "monotonously uneventful" in the frontier province.[10] Remote from the main centers of population, the settlers, mostly subsistence farmers, eked out an existence tilling fields or tending their flocks. These people endured a life that was grim. Clustered in villas, they lived in constant fear of Indian attacks, which were frequent. The New Mexico of the eighteenth century lacked wagon roads, canals, and navigable rivers. Trade was carried on by means of pack mules or *carretas* pulled by oxen over treacherous trails across a terrain fissured into countless canyons and arroyos, some as deep as a thousand feet. Up and down these stony chasms the traveler and his beasts of burden struggled as best they could. Contact with the outside world was slow in materializing.

The frontier remained closed to foreigners by royal decree until the Franco-Spanish competition for territory diminished after the end of the French and Indian War in 1763. In the meantime, New Mexicans had to satisfy themselves with goods produced locally or by Plains Indians, chiefly the Comanche. A trade fair held annually in Chihuahua took more than a month to get to by pack mules over the Chihuahua Trail. At Taos, the annual trade fair brought together Pueblos, Comanche, and Spaniards. In good years, all went well; in bad years, fighting sometimes broke out between the nomads and the settlers. Governors rarely had adequate soldiers to protect the settlers. The story of eighteenth-century New Mexico was essentially about security—protection from the elements and from the marauding nomadic tribes. In the words of Erna Fergusson:

---

9.   Ibid., p. 165.
10.   Beck, p. 89.

Security was what the *paisano* (peasant) coveted most. They knew the land and how to work it. Most importantly, they could distinguish between farming-land, grazing-land and land that would never be good for anything. For they came from semi-arid Mexico and Spain. Wherever they had lived, they had dug deep . . . and diverted streams and irrigating ditches.[11]

Factional strife was commonplace among the Pueblo Indians during the early years of the eighteenth century. According to Spicer, every pueblo was affected, with the probable exception of the Keres villages of Zia, Santa Ana, San Felipe, and some of the Tewas.[12] He goes on to say that the Tanos, who had surrendered to Governor Vargas, were for the most part distributed as slaves among the Spanish colonists. Those who were not so treated moved from Santa Fe out among the Tewa villages, principally to Tesuque. The resistant Tanos, who had been forced to Chimayo from their lands at Santa Cruz, and who had later participated in the 1694 and 1696 rebellions, migrated westward to take up residence among the Hopis. Some rebellious Tewas from San Ildefonso and other villages went westward to Hopi country. San Domingan survivors of the 1696 revolt, who had fought on the side of the Jemez, moved westward and founded a village called Laguna, not far from Acoma; some Jemez people migrated westward to the Hopi country.

During the early years of the 1700s, several thousand Pueblo Indians moved out of the Rio Grande valley, spurning Spanish control. They became known as the "apostates" and were regarded by the Spaniards as an obstacle to Spanish influence on the Hopis. In 1716, Governor Antonio Martinez decided to remove the threat of these apostates. He sent an expedition to bring them back, but he was only partly successful. He was even less successful in convincing the Tewa-speaking Tanos, who had settled on the mesa near the Hopi village of Walpi, to return.[13] There was much disagreement and strife among

---

11. Fergusson, *Our Southwest*, p. 247.
12. Spicer, p. 165.
13. Ibid.

the villagers within the pueblos in the Rio Grande valley. At Pecos, there was a strong anti-Spanish faction that was eventually silenced by the pro-Spanish leader, who executed five of the troublemakers. At San Ildefonso, lands that belonged to rebel Indians were given to pro-Spanish people from the Tewa village of Santa Clara. Throughout the area, the Spaniards were steadfastly encroaching on Indian lands. Cautiously, the Pueblos settled down and in a matter of time acceded to Spanish rule again.

The Missions

The death of Governor Vargas in 1704 marked the end of one phase of colonial New Mexican history and the opening of another. During the 1600s, the New Mexican colony had been essentially a government-subsidized Catholic mission domain for the Pueblo Indians under the direction of the Franciscan friars. Following the Pueblo Revolt and Spanish reconquest, the church's authority was substantially reduced. The crusade to stamp out the native religion was greatly modified, and measures previously used to curb the practice of native idol worship and witchcraft were, as a general rule, abandoned. Authorities tell us that the eighteenth century did not witness the renewal of the open discord that had marked relations between church and state during the preceding century, but there was still controversy.[14] For example, continuing maltreatment of the Indians by Spanish officials often put conversions at risk. The governor and most of his lieutenants looked on their positions of authority as a chance to improve their financial lot, and, as native labor constituted the only kind of economic wealth available, it was readily exploited.

The missions were self-supporting to a large extent from produce cultivated from the surrounding fields. Wheat, corn, and beans were the basic crops. Most friars raised fruit as well, and numerous references are made by travelers of the period to the fine orchards of peaches and apricots. Cotton was likewise grown where the climate would permit. Each mission had its own flock of sheep, and

14. Beck, p. 92.

some had herds of cattle and hogs. Frequently, the missions were little islands in the midst of a vast wilderness. Friars lived alone among the Indians, removed from contact with their fellow Spaniards and religious brethren. For the missionaries, it was a harsh life, cut off for long periods of time from contact with the outside world. It was not unusual for the priests to complain bitterly that they could not celebrate mass because the wine or the host was not available.[15]

Franciscans were rarely successful in their attempts to convert the Apaches. The desert tribes in the southwestern reaches of the territory, as far away as the Colorado River,[16] were more amenable. Jesuit padre Eusebio Francisco Kino, traveling on foot or by burro, had much greater success in converting the gentle Pima and Papago tribes. Both Jesuits and Franciscans tried unsuccessfully to convert the Hopis. When the missionaries arrived, the Hopis were adamant that they be allowed to worship in their own way. This was, of course, inconceivable to the eighteenth-century Spanish missionary mind. Friars thought that the natives desired conversion. The Navajos told Friar Juan Miguel Menchero that they "were grown up and could not become Christians because they had been raised like the deer." They were willing to "give some of the children to have water thrown upon them," but the elders would not become Christians. It was this deep conviction that made the friars' work so laborious among the Indian communities.[17]

ESTABLISHING FRONTIER COMMUNITIES

As New Mexico grew, there was an urgent need to establish communities farther from the Rio Grande valley and out into the frontier. Much of this expansion was made possible through a system of land grants that awarded tracts of land to individuals and groups who agreed to establish settlements and cultivate land beyond the Rio Grande valley.

---

15. Ibid., p. 91.
16. This was to be the western boundary of New Mexico until 1863, when Arizona was cut off as a separate territory.
17. Fergusson, *Three Peoples,* p. 187 (citing Henry W. Kelly, *Franciscan Missions of New Mexico*).

Communities were established at Santa Rosa de Lima to the north, San Miguel del Vado to the east, Cebolleta to the west, and Belen to the south. Prominent among those who shouldered the burden of frontier settlement and defense were the growing *mestizo* (mixed blood) population of the province. Among the least recognized of these groups were the Genízaro, Indians from various tribes who had, for a variety of reasons, lost their tribal identity. Many of them were captive children who had been raised in Spanish households, baptized, and given Spanish surnames. Genízaro settlements at Abiquiu and Tomé assumed much of New Mexico's frontier protection well into the nineteenth century. Notwithstanding many hardships, these communities expanded, contributing to the subsequent development and expansion of New Mexico.

NOMADIC INDIAN THREATS AND RETALIATORY CAMPAIGNS

New Mexico was literally surrounded by hostile tribes in the eighteenth century. Along its northern and eastern frontier were the Comanche and Jicarilla Apache; north and northwest were the Utes, who constantly fought with the Comanche; northwest and west were the Navajos; and southwest, south, and southeast were various other Apache tribes. While each of these tribes presented New Mexico with problems at various times during the century, it was the Comanche who posed the greatest threat to the colony's survival. Around 1706, this most warlike of all the Plains tribes began driving their hereditary enemies, the Apaches, out of the northeastern part of the province. Forty years later, the Comanches were the undisputed masters of the eastern plains region, having driven the Apaches to the west and south. Hardly a decade passed without settlements and pueblos being attacked.[18]

The Comanches could also be friendly. During periods of good behavior, they would attend the Taos fair, bringing with them some of their loot in the form of livestock, Indian slaves, or other goods to

18. Ibid., p. 94.

be traded for Spanish wares.[19] Regardless, the Spaniards made every effort to get rid of them. An expedition led by Don Juan de Padilla handed the tribe a crushing defeat in 1717. A similar setback was meted out in 1747. However, a steady campaign against the Comanches was difficult to conduct because many Spanish settlers found it advantageous to have them around, particularly for their trade. Even more important, the presence of the warlike Comanches in the plains established an effective buffer between the Spanish holdings in New Mexico and the French territory to the east. For that reason, a complete removal of this hostile tribe might not have been in the best interest of Spain.[20] In 1762, however, the French transferred what would become Louisiana to Spanish ownership and with it the policy toward the Comanches changed.

Spain's ambivalent attitude toward the Indians ended between 1775 and 1790, and a determined effort was made to control the Comanches and other nomadic tribes. In 1779, Juan Bautista de Anza (appointed governor in 1778) led a combined Spanish and Indian-ally force against the Comanches at Pueblo, Colorado, inflicting heavy losses on them and killing their chief, Cuerno Verde (Green Horn). However, Comanche raiding did not abate until 1786, when the Spanish government entered into a formal peace treaty with them.

The Apaches were a more merciless enemy of the Spaniards. The various tribes that made up the vast northern territory consistently raided the frontier settlements, killing or taking captives, driving off livestock, and spreading fear and devastation wherever they rode. The rugged terrain they occupied made it difficult for Spanish punitive expeditions to get at them, but as the raids became increasingly destructive and more daring, it became clear that Spain had to act decisively to rein in the predatory Apaches. To carry out this task, Spain was fortunate in having a series of competent military men, including General Don Hugo O'Conor, who initiated the campaign, and Governor Juan Bautista de Anza, who carried it out.[21]

---

19. Ibid. (citing Francisco Atanasio Dominguez, *Missions of New Mexico,* p. 252).
20. Ibid., p. 95.
21. Ibid., p. 96.

Don Juan Bautista de Anza, governor of New Mexico, 1778-88. (PAINTING BY FRAY ORSI, MEXICO CITY, 1774)

The action was relatively simple—chase the Apaches into their retreats, destroy their camps, and fight and kill them wherever possible. These search-and-destroy missions proved to be a formidable strategy against the Apaches. However, the Spaniards did not rely solely on military action to combat the Apaches. In the late 1780s, Viceroy Bernardo de Gálvez instituted an insidious scheme of chicanery. He ordered his military commanders to offer those Apaches who agreed to stop fighting free provisions in the form of "defective firearms, strong liquor and such other commodities as would render them militarily and economically dependent on the Spaniards."[22] This scheme, known as the Galvez Plan, was successful in bringing about an interim peace with the Apaches, and the so-called golden years followed (1790–1810), when the Apaches were more subdued than at any time previously. Yet, de Anza was less successful in making lasting peace with the Apaches than he had been with the Comanches. Some treaties were signed, but they were to be no more effective than those with the Americans almost a century later.[23]

FRENCH ENCROACHMENT

Intense rivalry between Spain and France for possession of the vast wilderness in the interior of North America began with French exploration of the Mississippi and Arkansas rivers in 1673. What followed was the establishment of French trapping outposts in Illinois country. In 1684, French explorer Robert Cavelier de la Salle set about colonizing the mouth of the Mississippi. Somehow, he missed his original destination and landed instead on the Texas coast in Spanish territory. La Salle's intrusion awakened the Spaniards, who sent several expeditions to intercept the intruders. By the time La Salle's site was discovered, it had been abandoned. However, the French intrusion, though negligible, was a signal to the Spaniards that New Spain's northern frontier was vulnerable to invaders. It was an area they had long claimed but had neglected to settle.

---

22. Lavin, p. 100 (citing Thomas E. Sheridan, *A History of the Southwest*, p. 37).
23. Lockwood, *The Apache Indians*, pp. 18–28.

The French, as accomplished traders, focused their attention on establishing a gainful commerce between their outposts and Santa Fe, but their attempts failed in 1724 and again in 1739. Impeding the initial efforts was the fact that the geography of the area was little understood. In 1748, Comanche traders at Taos reported that the rifles they carried had been purchased from French traders. This alarmed the Spaniards, for they took great care to keep firearms away from the Indians. During the next ten years, several parties of Frenchmen made their way either to Taos or to Santa Fe. Some of these unfortunate entrepreneurs were arrested and had their merchandise confiscated, as it was against Spanish economic policy throughout the colonial period for foreigners to trade with Spanish colonists.[24] Trade was a monopoly held by carefully selected merchants from Chihuahua, who had gained control of the former mission caravans and had dominated the commerce of New Mexico for much of the eighteenth century.

Franco-Spanish competition for territory in North America ended in 1763 with the end of the French and Indian War. In that conflict between England and France, France ended up losing most of her colonial empire on the American continent. Sensing the inevitable in 1762, the French ceded the vast Louisiana Territory to Spain to keep it from falling into English hands. With that windfall, the Spanish line of demarcation on the frontiers of New Mexico and Texas stretched all the way to the Mississippi. Since the militant English were still largely confined to the eastern seaboard beyond the Appalachians, the Spaniards could ignore, at least for the time being, any challenges from them.

PRESIDIAL REALIGNMENTS

Endorsed in Cayetano Marqués de Rubí's *Reglamento*[25] of 1772, major changes to New Spain's northern presidial system were carried out by

---

24. Beck, p. 98.
25. "The Marqués de Rubí's inspection of 1766–68 resulted in the *Reglamento é instrucciones para los presidios que han forman en la linea de frontera de la Nueva España* by King Carlos III on September 10, 1772, commonly called the Royal Regulations or New Regulations for Presidios, which authorized the building of fifteen presidios in a line from the Gulf of California to the Gulf of Mexico." (http://www.tsha.utexas.edu/handbook/online/articles/FF/qcf14.html)

Don Hugo O'Conor[26] when he was placed in charge of New Spain's entire northern frontier as commandant inspector in 1774. For the next six years, O'Conor traveled some twelve thousand miles on horseback, inspecting and realigning the frontier presidios. These presidial realignments were part of much broader reforms decreed by Spain's King Carlos III in 1776 (the year the American colonies revolted against England). He decreed that the border provinces of New Spain be removed from the jurisdiction of the viceroy in Mexico City and placed instead under the Spanish Crown through a newly created office that consolidated civil and military powers. At the same time, Spanish reformers toyed with the idea of abolishing the missions but abandoned the scheme as soon as it was realized that the missions were the cheapest and most effective way to control the Christianized Indians.

As the eighteenth century was drawing to a close, Spain's unstable hold on New Mexico was tenuous at best. The winds of social and economic change were fanning a new era. In the words of historian Thomas E. Sheridan:

> A new order had arisen in northern New Spain, one that reflected a fundamental change in European society and the colonies Europe controlled. The world economy was growing more and more capitalistic as medieval privileges crumbled. Consequently, resources such as land and labor became commodities in the marketplace rather than rights and duties locked up in a feudal order. The Jesuit dream of independent missions contradicted the entrepreneurial dream of abundant land and a mobile labor force. With the Jesuits gone and the Franciscans weakened, it became much easier for Spanish settlers to exploit that land and labor for private use.[27]

---

26. Hugo O'Conor was born in Dublin in December 1734.
27. Thomas E. Sheridan, *Arizona: A History*, p. 36.

CHAPTER SEVEN

From Spanish Province to Part of the United States

As the nineteenth century began, Spain's precarious hold in New Mexico was fast drawing to a close. Titular ownership soon was to pass to Mexico, but there was only to be a pause until the westward sweep of Manifest Destiny would bring the Anglo-Americans into possession.

—Warren A. Beck, *New Mexico: A History of Four Centuries*

Mexico gained its independence from Spain in 1821, bringing to a close three centuries of Spanish rule on the North American continent and making New Mexico a part of the Mexican Republic, an area larger than British North America (Canada) and the (then) United States.

From the turn of the nineteenth century until the end of Spanish rule in North America, European power struggles played a larger and more frequent role in shaping the course of events in New Mexico than had previously been the case. These events more or less began in 1808, when Spain's ruling aristocracy became the unwilling hosts to an army of French troops who expelled their monarch and proclaimed Napoleon's brother Joseph their king. In New Spain, this alarming chain of events aroused conflicting sentiments. To many of the *criollos* (native-born Mexicans), who were intensely hostile toward their peninsular (Spanish-born) leaders, it was finally the moment to grab the reins of power and establish an independent Mexico. A whole network of criollo groups throughout the provinces plotted for independence; opposing them were the powerful Spanish overlords who ran the government, army, and church. From the time Napoleon upset the Spanish monarchy, New Spain's criollo and peninsular factions challenged each other for dominance. Meanwhile, in Mexico City, two viceroys were brought down in rapid succession by coups d'état.

REVOLUTION AND INDEPENDENCE

Mexico's struggle for separation from the motherland actually began on September 16, 1810, when Father Miguel Hidalgo led a rebellion to free his country from colonial rule. Haplessly, not everyone went along. Although Hidalgo was killed and his rebellion crushed, the Hidalgo Revolt planted the seeds of self-determination. Following a decade of bloody encounter, Mexico won its independence from Spain in 1821 and declared itself a republic in 1824.

Politically, New Mexico was a province until 1824, when its status changed to that of a territory. In 1836, it became a department and remained so until the end of Mexican rule. Although the boundaries were never defined, the Department of New Mexico included what are now the states of Arizona and New Mexico, as well as areas of Colorado, Utah, and Nevada.[1] Its capital at Santa Fe numbered 4,500 inhabitants, and numerous cattle ranches flourished in its fertile eastern lands (present-day New Mexico). In marked contrast, all the ranches in the western portion (present-day Arizona) had been abandoned, leaving only the settlements of Tubac and Tucson, each guarded by a small garrison. Throughout the early years of the young republic, almost every institution that had held the Spanish frontier together disintegrated as the country plunged into civil war and bankruptcy. The federal Congress passed a law in 1827, compelling Spanish-born people to leave the country. In conformity with the national law, several states enacted similar legislation. The clergy were required to take a loyalty oath to Mexico; those who refused were expelled. Church lands were confiscated and auctioned to the highest bidder. During the turmoil of the revolutionary years, the silver mining industry was

---

1.   Beck, p. 120.

abandoned, the national treasury was almost depleted, and, along the northern frontier, funds that had maintained missions, presidios, and Apache peace camps dried up.

Peace agreements with Apaches were ignored during the revolutionary years, and raiding broke out again. In a frantic move to control the Apaches, the states of Chihuahua and Sonora decided on a war of extermination by offering bounties on Apache scalps. The program, called Projecto de Guerra, attracted an assortment of bloodthirsty ruffians who organized into units and rode into Apacheria[2] in search of their "quarry." This genocidal crusade continued at a vigorous pace throughout the 1830s, although at times bounty funds were in short supply to pay for all the scalps being brought in. No one really knows how many Apaches were killed by the scalp hunters; the policy, barbaric and immoral as it was, served only to intensify the savagery and make the Apache warriors more relentlessly warlike.[3]

Some Anglo-American trappers and traders entered into this trade along with the Mexicans. Unconscionably, they found it more lucrative to "trap for hair than for fur," and, as one wag put it, "caring naught whether they scalped the Mexicans themselves."[4] Any scalp, Indian or other, brought the pledged bounty. It was a time of treachery, violence, and bloodshed, and it instigated a recurrence of savage Apache warfare. For several years after the revolution had begun, Mexico experienced one unstable government after another, until one man, Antonio López de Santa Anna, finally wrested control of the government and entrenched himself as president-dictator. In 1835, he returned the country to a strong central government, usurping some of the powers that individual states, including Texas, had enjoyed since the revolution. This worsened relations between American colonists in Texas and the Mexican government and led to the Mexican-American War of 1846 (as well as to the subsequent acquisition of the Southwest from Texas to California). The Spaniards had long been

---

2.   A strip of territory roughly 250 miles wide, from Casa Grande to Zuni, which separated the Sonora-Chihuahua part of the frontier from the New Mexico part, controlled by the Apaches.

3.   Lavin, p. 118.

4.   Ibid.

haunted by the dread that other European powers were plotting to invade their sparsely populated northern frontier, but for the Mexicans who had won independence from Spain, it was the United States that made those fears a reality.

ZEBULON PIKE EXPEDITION

In the decades before New Spain won independence in 1821, her northern frontier endured another challenge, one posed by American interlopers. One of the first who braved it across the plains country was twenty-six-year-old Lieutenant Zebulon Pike, who led a small party into New Mexico in 1806.

Washington was then beginning to pay increased attention to Spanish America. Three years before, Spain (under pressure from Napoleon) returned Louisiana to France with the understanding that the territory would not be delivered into the hands of a third power.[5] The restriction was completely ignored by Napoleon, who turned about-face and sold the entire Louisiana Territory to the United States. For New Spain, as well as for the United States, the immediate problem was one of boundaries. It was not clearly set out where the north, west, and south limits of Louisiana were. Lacking any governing rules, both countries vied for the same territory, the United States asserting rights over all lands extending to the Rio Grande, and Spain claiming the Missouri River as the northern boundary of New Mexico and Texas.

In the spring of 1807, Pike led his party over the mountains to the Rio Grande where, near the mouth of the Rio Conejos, he raised the Stars and Stripes over a building that his men had constructed. His belief that he was on American soil was dispelled when a Spanish force from Santa Fe descended on the remote little post. Escorted to the New Mexican capital, Pike was subjected to prolonged questioning by Governor Joaquin del Real Alencaster and his aides regarding the motives of his expedition. Displeased with the answers, the governor ordered Pike and his men taken to Chihuahua (a six-hundred-mile

---

5.   Simmons, *Interpretive History,* p. 96.

Lt. Zebulon M. Pike, 1779-1813.

journey) for further interrogation by the commandant general of Spanish forces in Northern Mexico, General Nemesio Salcedo, who confiscated their maps and official documents. In June 1807, they were finally released and deported into American territory at Natchitoches, Louisiana.[6] On his return, Pike wrote a report of his travels and experiences in New Mexico, which was published in 1810. This work gave Americans their first exposure to Hispanic life and customs along the Rio Grande and stirred an interest in the area.[7]

After Pike had shown the way, several Americans attempted to trade with the isolated province and to fish in its streams. In general, these efforts were futile until after 1821, when a combination of circumstances stemming from the success of the Mexican Revolution led to a relaxation of trade restrictions on foreigners. Up to that time, New Mexicans had been denied the opportunity of dealing with English- and French-speaking traders from the East. Under Mexican rule, this protectionist policy was replaced and foreigners were at liberty to enter the province for the purpose of trade. This open trade policy ushered in a new era of commerce along the Santa Fe Trail that spanned an area from Independence, Missouri, into territory that eventually became the states of Oklahoma, Texas, and New Mexico. This trade expanded the limits of the vast frontier and increased the flow of Americans into the Southwest.

In the same year that Mexico won its independence, Captain William Becknell (a famed Indian fighter and veteran of the War of 1812) and four companions went out from Arrow Head, Missouri, to Santa Fe by the far western prairie route. The country beyond Missouri was a vast uncharted land where few white men had ventured and few returned of those who did. Beyond the plains lay the desert, and further ahead impassable mountains separated them from the Santa Fe they hoped to reach. As Becknell started on his trip, there were events happening far to the south in Mexico City that would greatly influence the future course of the American West. The joint revolutionary forces of Agustin de Iturbide and Vincente Guerrero, known as the Trigarante army, had captured Mexico from the

6.   Ibid., p. 99.
7.   Beck, p. 103.

Spaniards and declared a vast area of the continent from Oregon in the north to Panama in the south an independent nation. Becknell and his party were unaware of this when, on November 13 at Rock River, they were intercepted by a party of Mexican rangers who, instead of detaining them, prevailed upon them to continue their journey to Santa Fe where they disposed of their merchandise at a handsome profit.[8] The favorable reports brought back by Becknell stimulated others to embark in trade, including Colonel Cooper, who, accompanied by several others from Becknell's neighborhood in Franklin, Missouri, hauled a consignment of merchandise to Taos the following year.[9] The success of these trading missions encouraged others to follow suit. The United States, understanding the importance of this trade, opened a consular office in Santa Fe in 1825. That same year, Senator Thomas H. Benton introduced a bill in Congress to authorize the building of a road from Missouri through Indian country to the borders of New Mexico. The bill passed Congress and was signed into law by President Monroe before he left office.[10] This road served as an international thoroughfare between the United States and the Republic of Mexico for a quarter of a century.

The hazards of the trip were many: animals often stampeded for no reason or were driven off by Indians, and the elements frequently took their toll. But the most frightening hazards of all came from encounters with "thirst and the red man."[11] Yet, many venturesome entrepreneurs made their fortunes moving merchandise and driving livestock over the Santa Fe Trail while others, equally daring, lost their life savings and, on occasion, their lives.

The result of the Santa Fe trade on New Mexico was both instantaneous and lasting. In effect, the once-isolated settlements went through an economic transformation. Not only were imported consumer goods now available for local consumption, but also New Mexicans were purchasing goods from the Americans and sending them

---

8. Gregg, *The Commerce of the Prairies*, pp. 6–7.
9. For the complete story of the Santa Fe Trail, see Josiah Gregg's *The Commerce of the Prairies*, a narrative of the author's recollections of his ten years (1831–1841) spent on the Santa Fe Trail.
10. Gregg, *Commerce*, p. 12.
11. Gregg, *Commerce*, p. 59.

southward to Chihuahua and westward to California. During the years between 1833 and 1844, more than half of the cargo entering Santa Fe was sent southward. In time, Santa Fe became the port of entry for supplying the markets of Chihuahua and California and, at the same time, provided the New Mexico authorities with most of the revenue to run the province.[12] Unfortunately, the Santa Fe trade brought discord between the Americans and the New Mexicans. Warren Beck describes how much of this ill feeling came from the traditional Spanish fear of interlopers, foreigners, and Protestants. A constant source of irritation to the Americans was the whimsical manner in which the Mexican laws were applied. As the caravans entered Santa Fe, the traders never knew whether the custom fees were going to be modest or exorbitant, the amount often decided by the current status of the local treasury or the immediate needs of New Mexico's governor.

Beck suggests the antagonism was not all caused by the New Mexicans. Most Americans entering Santa Fe were Protestants who carried with them the predisposed prejudice of the day toward the Roman Catholic faith, and many seldom missed an opportunity to reveal it.[13] Anti-American resentment was stirred up also by the ill-fated Texan Santa Fe Expedition in 1841 and the subsequent Texas reprisals, which were cause for all Anglos to be suspected of conniving to seize the province (described later in the chapter). Mexican authorities, fearing the ever-growing number of Americans who were moving into New Mexico, attempted to cut off the Santa Fe trade after the secession of Texas. But New Mexico needed American goods too badly, and the embargoes were not effective. The Mexican-American War of 1846 caused an almost complete collapse of normal trade on the trail, but the needs of the military led to the continuation of the caravans. Once the war was over, the old trade was renewed and, along with it, a regular passenger service, using stagecoaches, emerged. Then came the railroad, shortening the trail and pushing the eastern terminus farther westward until finally, in 1879, the railroad reached New Mexico, putting an end to the Santa Fe trade era.

---

12. Beck, p. 116.
13. Ibid.

Anglo-American Mountain Men

As traders began to push their way westward along the Santa Fe Trail, parties of trappers (or "mountain men," as they were generally called) were scouring the Rocky Mountains for beaver pelts. The story of these mountain men, however, is not one that belongs to the history of New Mexico alone. While their base of operations might have been at Taos or Bent's Fort, the entire west was theirs to explore at will. Few writers capture their lifestyle more fittingly than Erna Fergusson:

> From Canada to Mexico they trapped beaver on every creek, followed every river, crossed every divide, learned to avoid every precipice and to shelter in every cave. . . . As scouts they showed old moccasin-worn trails to such "pathfinders" as Frémont and Kearny. Then as soldiers, even as officers, they proved invaluable to the country they had never dreamt of changing for another. . . . Perhaps, the archetype of such men was New Mexico's Kit Carson, the illiterate boy who ran away from an apprenticeship in Missouri and became a legend in his lifetime."[14]

According to Warren Beck, those who sought the beaver along New Mexico's mountain streams were typically the most rugged individuals of the American frontier. With little more than a small supply of salt, gunpowder, some knives, a gun, and the necessary traps, they headed out after the spring thaw and worked until June. With their pack animals laden with pelts, they headed back to their base of operations where they traded their catch. After a period of revelry, and an ensuing period of unwinding, they picked up their needed supplies and headed out again in the fall to renew the hunt. During the winter, some trappers lived with the Indians where they frequently had native wives.[15]

The first Anglo-American mountain men arrived in New Mexico in the early 1820s. They were, as historian Thomas E. Sheridan so

---

14. Fergusson, *Three Peoples,* p. 238.
15. Beck, pp. 106–107.

aptly described them, a ragtag collection of misfits, adventurers, and businessmen who entered the territory for one purpose and one purpose only: to trap the "hairy banknotes," as they called beavers, from every watercourse between the Rio Grande and the Colorado delta.[16] Among the first known to set foot in the wilderness regions of the Southwest were James Pratt and his father, Sylvester, who spent the winter of 1825–1826 trapping along the San Francisco, Gila, and San Pedro rivers. They had left their family farm in Kentucky in 1824 and headed for St. Louis, where they outfitted themselves for a fur-trapping expedition. Arriving in Taos in the fall of 1825, they first had to secure permission from the New Mexican authorities, as well as obtain a Mexican license, before heading into the province in search of their hairy banknotes.

They ran into the usual temporary delay as the Mexican authorities, unhappy with the increasing number of buckskin Yankees entering their territory, were restricting the number of licenses they were issuing. In due course, however, the Pratts and their friends, licenses in hand, were on their way. They followed the Rio Grande south to Socorro, then headed west to the Santa Rita del Cobre mines—the last outpost of Spanish civilization—resting before going into the rugged Gila hinterland, where their trapping netted several thousand dollars worth of pelts, which they hauled back to Santa Fe.

During the winter of 1826–1827, James Pratt returned to New Mexico to join a group of French trappers led by Miguel Robideau, one of six brothers who had grown up trapping along the Missouri River. Together, they journeyed down the Gila to the junction of the Salt and Gila rivers, where they stopped at a village of Spanish-speaking Papago Indians, who, according to some sources, may have been Yavapais or Tonto Apaches. The villagers invited the trappers to stay the night, all of whom accepted with the exception of a suspicious Pratt, who camped some distance away. As Pratt tells it, that evening the natives turned their war clubs on their guests, killing all but Robideau, an unidentified Frenchman, and Pratt himself. Fleeing the massacre, the three stumbled on the camp of another group of trappers led by Ewing Young. Young, a hard-bitten mountain man

---

16. Sheridan, *Arizona: A History*, p. 42.

who, it is said, feared neither man nor beast, led his men back to the village where they exacted revenge. When it was all over, according to Pratt, more than one hundred Indians had been slaughtered. Pratt remained with Young's outfit for the rest of the season, trapping up and down the Salt and Verde rivers. The group then followed the Gila to Yuma Crossing, becoming the first Anglo-Americans to make the trek.[17] In 1830, James Pratt returned to his old Kentucky home, where he related astonishing stories of his encounters with New Mexico's "fierce human and animal inhabitants," battling with grizzlies, mountain lions, and Apaches and braving Comanche arrows to rescue naked women and surviving a harrowing desert ordeal. Other trappers may have preceded the Pratts, but many others certainly followed them, venturing into the unexplored valleys and mountains of the Territory of New Mexico, trapping and hunting in pursuit of a living. Fortunately, no other encounter between mountain men and Indians measured up to the horror of the Robideau massacre or its revenge. Nevertheless, there were frequent encounters as mountain men trekked through Apacheria or trapped beaver in Mohave territory along the Colorado. To the Native Americans, they were armed intruders who had entered their lands without permission to snatch beaver from their rivers and streams. As their numbers increased, bands of Apache and Yavapai warriors intensified their resistance to these incursions. By the late 1830s, most mountain men avoided Apacheria.

REVOLT OF 1837

Following independence, most of New Mexico's governors, appointed by the national government, were selected from a handful of local families who dominated provincial politics. That changed in 1835, when Colonel Albino Pérez, an officer in the Mexican army and an "outsider," was sent to Santa Fe to assume the governor's seat.[18] At the same time, Mexico carried out a reorganization of its national

---

17. Lavin, pp. 119–121.
18. Simmons, *Interpretive History*, pp. 112–113.

government and established a system of direct taxation. New Mexicans, who had been accustomed to administering their own affairs and collecting revenue from the Santa Fe trade, were bitterly displeased. Their displeasure ignited a full-scale rebellion (customarily termed the Chimayo Rebellion) in 1837.

Historian Warren Beck suggests that the initial cause of the revolt was a misconstrued debt-collection problem in the form of a suit brought to collect a debt of one hundred pesos. When judgment was handed down for the defendants, who were relatives of the *alcalde* (local official), an appeal to the prefect set aside the finding. Somehow, this was misread by the citizens as a decision in favor of taxation.[19] Responding to the cry of "taxes, taxes," farming folk and Pueblo Indians joined forces and descended on Santa Fe in protest. According to Josiah Gregg's recollections,[20] "Governor Pérez issued orders to the *alcaldes* for the assembling of the militia; but all that could be collected together was about a hundred and fifty men, including warriors of the Pueblo of Santo Domingo. With this inadequate force the Governor made an attempt to march from the capital, but was soon surprised by the insurgents, who lay in ambush near La Cañada." According to Gregg, the governor's forces were chased back to the city, where the rebels captured Pérez and put him and several of his aides to death. The rebels then installed a mestizo named José Gonzalez (one of their own) from Ranchos de Taos as provisional governor.

However, the revolution was short-lived. Former governor Manuel Armijo raised a small force and marched on the capital; Governor Gonzalez, without an army to support him, fled north. Armijo proclaimed himself governor and *comandante general* and dispatched a courier to Mexico City with the news. In the meantime, news of the insurrection had reached the authorities in Mexico City, who ordered some three hundred troops from Chihuahua to New Mexico. Arriving at Santa Fe in January 1838, these troops, together with Governor Armijo's little army, marched against the rebels (who by this time had again regrouped in sizable numbers) and soundly defeated them. Deposed governor José Gonzalez was later captured and executed.

---

19. Beck, p. 122.
20. Gregg, *Commerce*, pp. 122–123.

General Manuel Armijo, governor of New Mexico. (PASTEL AND CHARCOAL DRAWING, 1845)

As this uprising occurred shortly after Texas had ceded from Mexico, American merchants everywhere were accused of being the instigators of this insurrection. Their goods were confiscated or sequestered upon the slightest pretext and, as Josiah Gregg describes it, "these and other indignities were heaped upon them as a punishment for the occurrence of events which it had not been in their power to prevent."[21] According to some sources, this mistaken impression was strengthened when the Indian rebels denied allegiance to Mexico and proposed that a deputation asking for protection be sent to Texas.[22]

Texan Expedition into New Mexico

New Mexico had no sooner returned to normal following the 1837 revolt when another episode provided added problems for Anglo-Americans trying to do business in New Mexico. A wagon train of 270 Texans, led by General Hugh McLeod, approached New Mexico in 1841, claiming their visit was to engage in peaceful commerce. The Mexican government, not unexpectedly, chose to look at it as an unfriendly incursion, and Governor Armijo began preparations to ensure that the province did not fall into the hands of the Texans.

Whatever their motive, the Texans never reached Santa Fe. Exhausted and starved from the 1,300-mile inhospitable journey through an Indian-infested waterless land of every conceivable terrain, and deceived by the treachery of one of their members, they were captured by Governor Armijo's forces and subjected to the most brutal treatment "ever meted out in the history of warfare."[23] Many expedition members were shot down in cold blood; others were cruelly tortured, and most of them were forced into a death march southward to Mexico City. Once in Mexico City, they were subjected to various indignities and cruelties before being released the following year.[24]

---

21. Ibid., p. 126.
22. Beck, p. 122.
23. Ibid., p. 126.
24. Ibid., p. 127 (citing Thomas Falconer, *Letters and Notes on the Expedition,* p. 215).

The legacy of the Texan Santa Fe debacle was to linger on. The brutal treatment of the helpless prisoners angered the Texans, but the Republic of Texas was in no position to do anything about it. Its treasury was in dire financial condition; public debt was more than seven million dollars, and there was insufficient money to pay even the interest on it. Furthermore, Governor Armijo's military success toughened Mexican attitudes toward the Texans, inspiring the launch of an attempted reconquest of the breakaway Republic of Texas in 1842. In that year, Mexican forces captured San Antonio and plundered the town before being driven off. In addition, a Mexican force seized Corpus Christi. Such actions forced Republic president Sam Houston to send retaliatory forces against the Mexicans. In June 1843, Texan forces under Colonel Jacob Snively encountered an advance guard of Mexicans on the Santa Fe Trail and, in the ensuing fight, killed eighteen of them and captured about eighty more.[25]

The annexation of Texas by the United States in 1845 was viewed by Mexico as an act of war, and Mexico reacted by cutting off diplomatic relations. This was followed by a dispute over the international boundary, unpaid claims owed by Mexico to American citizens, and, in the belief of many historians, U.S. President James Polk's expansionary drive of Manifest Destiny. When an offer to purchase the Southwest area was rejected, the Polk administration looked for a ploy to take the region by force. It would come soon enough in the disputed lands between the Nueces River and the Rio Grande.

---

25. Ibid., p. 128.

CHAPTER EIGHT

The United States Takes Control

The capture of New Mexico figured in President Polk's expansion plans mainly because it was on the path to California. To effect its capture, an army was organized at Fort Leavenworth under Stephen Watts Kearney.

—Warren A. Beck, *New Mexico: A History of Four Centuries*

A quarter century of Mexican rule in New Mexico ended in August of 1846 when Brigadier General Stephen Watts Kearney and his Army of the West marched over the Santa Fe Trail into New Mexico's undefended northern frontier and took possession of the territory. Three months earlier, the United States Congress had declared war on Mexico over long-standing difficulties between the two nations. Unquestionably, the move was motivated by the country's expansionist drive of Manifest Destiny, which had been given new emphasis in 1845 when John L. Sullivan, writing in the *New York Morning News*, stated: "Our manifest destiny is to overspread and possess the whole continent which providence has given us for the . . . great expectations of liberty."[1]

Whatever cause is attributed to the conflict, dubbed the Mexican-American War, its seeds were sown in 1824 when Mexico invited Anglo-Americans and other foreign colonists to settle the sparsely populated lands of Texas. This colonization was so successful that, by the mid-1830s, American settlers had surpassed Mexicans by a ratio of ten to one. When a group of colonists seized a Mexican fort at

---

1. Simmons, *Interpretive History*, p. 120 (quoting from T. R. Fehrenbach, *The Comanches: Destruction of a People*, p. 363).

Anahuac, the move for separation from Mexico was set in motion. A group of settlers met and adopted a declaration of independence from Mexico in 1836 and shortly thereafter defeated a Mexican army under Santa Anna at the Battle of San Jacinto. The settlers immediately ratified their own constitution and sent an envoy to Washington to seek annexation to the United States or recognition as the independent Republic of Texas. Indeed, Texas remained an independent republic until 1845, when it was finally annexed to the United States.

In the meantime, President Polk, hoping to acquire the great stretch of land from Texas to California by diplomatic negotiation with Mexico, sent John Slidell to Mexico City to discuss its purchase. When the Mexican government refused to parley, Polk began to look for a pretext to take the area by force. He did not have to wait long. Mexican troops crossed the lower Rio Grande and engaged a U.S. reconnaissance party in a cavalry skirmish on soil claimed by the United States in April 1846. Polk now had all the justification he needed, and the war was on. Further attacks by Mexican forces led to the United States blockading Mexican ports on the Pacific Ocean and in the Gulf of Mexico. An army under General Winfield Scott was sent to Vera Cruz by sea with orders to advance on Mexico City. A second army under General Zachary Taylor entered Mexico from Texas, while a third army, the Army of the West under the command of Colonel Stephen Watts Kearny, was ordered to take Santa Fe and then march to California.

INVASION OF NEW MEXICO

Manual Armijo was governor of the Department of New Mexico in 1846 when the Army of the West marched on Santa Fe. He also had been governor in 1828, but his real power came in 1837 when he proclaimed himself both governor and *comandante general* after successfully ending the revolt by Santa Cruz de la Cañada pueblo. Four years later, in 1841, he had succeeded in halting the ill-fated Texan "invasion" of New Mexico. However, he encountered numerous problems during his years as governor, including disloyalty from the citizens, intimidation from hostile Indians, threats of a gringo invasion,

General Stephen W. Kearny (1847).

and lack of sufficient funds to run his province. He had warned the Mexican government in 1840 against Anglo-American intrusions, citing such outposts as Bent's Fort east of the Arkansas River as "the protection of robbers, either foreigners or Mexicans."[2] As it turned out, his anxieties were justified. In 1846, General Kearney addressed a proclamation from Bent's Fort to Armijo: "I come by orders of my government to take possession of the country over part of which you are now presiding as governor." Kearney then crossed the Arkansas River into Mexican territory.[3]

Stephen Watts Kearney (a veteran of the War of 1812) was no novice when he was named brigadier general and commander of the Army of the West in 1845. He was familiar with the West from Yellowstone to Bent's Fort. His army, which consisted of three hundred regular cavalry, eight hundred rowdy, undisciplined but tough volunteers from Missouri, and a battalion of Mormons whose mission was to build a road across New Mexico, entered Santa Fe on August 18, 1846, and took possession of the city.

It was an occupation accomplished through a mixture of diplomacy and cunning, much as Diego de Vargas had done during the Spanish *reconquista* of 1692. According to one version, an adroit Kearny sent one of his officers, Captain Phillip St. George Cooke, ahead on a secret mission to Governor Armijo. Accompanying him was James W. Magoffin, who had engaged in the Santa Fe trade for many years. Magoffin, an Irish Catholic married to a Mexican woman, mixed easily with the native population. One writer described him as a "smooth-talking Irishman with a well-stocked mind, a genial host with a well-stocked cellar and a sound patriot."[4] Senator Benton of Missouri had introduced Magoffin to President Polk and to Secretary of War Marcy, after which both agreed that he should go west with the army. What else was agreed on is not known, nor is it known what Magoffin discussed with his friend, Governor Armijo, during their secret meeting in Santa Fe. Evidently, he succeeded in convincing Armijo (or buying him off) not to resist Kearney's men. As some

2.   Fergusson, *Three Peoples,* p. 251.
3.   Ibid.
4.   Ibid., p. 249.

Raising the American flag over the Governor's Palace, Santa Fe, New Mexico, August 18, 1846. (DRAWING BY KENNETH CHAPMAN, 1915)

General Stephen W. Kearny delivering proclamation at Las Vegas, New Mexico on August 15, 1846.

historians tell it, Armijo and his force of dragoons had conveniently fled Santa Fe southward to Albuquerque, and ultimately to Chihuahua, by the time the Army of the West entered Santa Fe on August 18, 1846, capturing the capital without a single shot being fired.[5] The story behind Armijo's defection has been the subject of much conjecture by historians. Some believe Magoffin bought him off in hard cash. Others suggest that he had never effectively led troops in battle and was widely suspected of being a coward. Erna Fergusson cites a letter of August 26, 1848, stating that "Armijo's officers had pulled out with auxiliaries, leaving the Governor nothing to do but retire."[6]

Upon entering the capital, General Kearney raised the Stars and Stripes over the palace of the governor and read a proclamation declaring that the Territory of New Mexico was from then on part of the United States. He told those gathered that he had come as a friend, guaranteeing them self-government, freedom of religion, and the other advantages of United States citizenship.[7] Kearney then set about organizing the first Anglo-American form of government for the territory. He appointed Charles Bent as acting governor and instructed Francis Preston Blair Jr. to draft a code of law, the Kearny Code, which combined Mexican and Anglo-American law and set forth provisions for a governor, a court system, and a legislature.[8]

Kearney's march into New Mexico was uneventful; he had captured a vast territory without firing a shot. By a proclamation spoken in English to a people who did not understand the language, New Mexico was declared part of the United States, and all who opposed the idea were branded traitors. Ironically, it was the trade that had so benefited New Mexico that was the most important dynamic in preparing the way for conquest by the United States. The Santa Fe trade had turned New Mexico northward, away from Mexico.

---

5. Beck, p. 132 (citing a footnote to Bancroft, *History of Arizona and New Mexico, 1530–1888*, p. 412, describing how Colonel Magoffin later claimed $50,000 from the United States but was able to collect only $30,000).
6. Fergusson, *Three Peoples*, p. 254 (citing Mexican historian José María Roa Barcena as her source).
7. Beck, p. 133.
8. Blair, a member of a distinguished political family, served in Congress from Missouri and was later an officer in the Civil War.

Charles Bent, first governor of New Mexico under the United States.

Commercially, New Mexico had been occupied by the United States long before 1846. The path to conquest, soon to be traveled by the American army, had been shaped by the wagons of the traders. On the eve of the war, international trade over the Santa Fe Trail had reached one-third of a million dollars, a far cry from the thirty men carrying three hundred dollars in merchandise who had opened the trade in 1821.

TAOS REBELLION AGAINST THE U.S. MILITARY

New Mexicans did not live under the Kearny Code for long. Despite the outside appearance of having accepted the Americans, many New Mexicans, Hispanics, and Indians nurtured a deep resentment toward the invaders, which would soon express itself in a general revolt. A variety of factors contributed to the general dissatisfaction. First, some leading New Mexicans were unhappy with the new government; they felt Kearny had appointed too many Anglo-American officeholders. Some Indians had shared power during the Mexican period, but there were only two among Kearny's appointees. Leading New Mexicans were also unhappy, simply because they disliked the United States. There was also a fear among Hispanics and Pueblo Indians that they would lose their lands or that their lands would be taxed.[9]

While the Americans set about organizing a new government in the ancient capital of Santa Fe, plans were being hatched to rid New Mexico of its latest conquerors in a series of meetings in Santa Fe during December 1848. Rumors of an impending uprising reached the authorities in late December, leading to the arrest of several suspected leaders. But these measures did little to suppress the escalating unrest. On January 19, 1847, a mob of Indians forced its way into the Taos home of Charles Bent, the recently appointed governor, and murdered him in the presence of his wife and children. The mob then went through the whole town, breaking into houses and slaying every American they could lay their hands on, hunting down Mexicans who had taken office under the new American government and harassing those known to be friendly with the Americans.

---

9.   Roberts, p. 211.

News of the Taos uprising reached Colonel Price at Santa Fe on January 20, and he quickly mustered an assorted force of some five hundred soldiers, former mountain men, and, ironically, several Mexicans who had just been released from jail for their participation in the December Santa Fe plot.[10] They marched north through heavy snow and bitter cold. At Santa Cruz de la Cañada on January 24, they encountered and decisively beat a 1,500-strong force of insurgents. Revolts at Embudo and Mora were similarly suppressed.

After further defeats, the rebels retreated to Taos, where they set up a defensive position at the Church of San Jeronimo. There, after two days of intense fighting, the insurgents were finally overcome. Many prisoners were taken, and a series of tragic trials followed, at which a number of the survivors were tried and sentenced to death for crimes of murder and treason. The charge of treason raised objections. How could a Mexican citizen (who had not at that time been granted United States citizenship) be guilty of treason? It turned out that Francis Preston Blair, the prosecuting attorney, was of the mistaken impression that Kearney had granted blanket citizenship and did not understand that such action required the acceptance of the Peace Treaty by Washington.[11]

The war with Mexico ended with the signing of the Treaty of Guadalupe Hidalgo in 1848. New Mexico was securely *in* the United States, but, as one observer noted, it would be a long time before New Mexico would be *part* of the United States. The nomadic tribes remained a menace, raiding settlements and stealing livestock and crops. In contrast, the Pueblo tribes settled down after the Taos revolt, fully accepting the new allegiance.

NEW MEXICO DESIGNATED A U.S. TERRITORY

The war with Mexico ended in 1848 with the signing of the Treaty of Guadalupe Hidalgo near Mexico City. Mexico agreed to give up its claims to Texas and ceded nearly half of her territory to the United

---

10. Beck, p. 137.
11. Ibid., p. 138.

States, including California, New Mexico, Nevada, Utah, and Colorado. Two years later, on September 9, 1850, the U.S. Congress passed an Organic Act, creating the Territory of New Mexico, an area consisting of present-day New Mexico, Arizona, parts of southern Colorado, southern Utah, and even a portion of southeast Nevada.

In 1851, a territorial government was set up, and officials appointed the governor, district judges, and U.S. district attorneys. Self-government was placed in a bicameral legislative assembly, the members of which were elected by their respective districts. Laws enacted could be, and on occasion were, invalidated by the Congress of the United States. As most of the legislators were Spanish speaking, an interpreter was needed.

Boundary Disputes and Adjustments

Once General Kearney and the Army of the West had accomplished what the Texans were unable to do—that is, conquer New Mexico—the Lone Star State was only too eager to press its territorial claim westward to the Rio Grande. Acceptance of the Texas claim would have meant the inclusion of Santa Fe within Texas. As Santa Fe was the capital of the province under the Spanish-colonial governors long before Texas was settled by "anything but scorpions and Indians," the claim appeared all the more absurd.[12] Texas had strongly asserted her claim during the course of the war but had awaited final disposition of the matter pending the peace treaty. In 1848, the Texas legislature passed a series of laws creating a county organization with a supporting governing system for the Santa Fe area, appointing one Spruce M. Baird to serve as judge and supervisor of the newly created county.

Upon his arrival, the people of Santa Fe gave Baird a chilly reception. The Santa Fe military-controlled newspaper declared: "There is not a citizen, either American or Mexican, that will ever acknowledge themselves as citizens of Texas. . . . New Mexico does not belong, nor has Texas ever had a right to claim her as a part of Texas. . . . Texas

---

12. Ibid., p. 141.

should show some little sense, and drop this question."[13] New Mexico was still under military rule, although efforts were underway to set up a civil government. There were those who hoped for admission to the Union as a state; others were satisfied with territorial status. This kept matters in such an uproar that nobody was interested in Mr. Baird's agenda. New Mexicans, more interested in achieving statehood than yielding to the regime in Austin, issued a proclamation in the spring of 1850, calling for a constitutional convention on the question of statehood. Texans were aghast; many were of the opinion that the situation had now reached a point at which their claims should be enforced by military action. Others, believing these claims to have been sanctioned when Texas was admitted to the Union, demanded that annexation be rescinded if the demands were not met. When the Texan delegation in Congress protested to the Taylor administration, they were politely told that New Mexico always had the right to petition for statehood, and, further, the boundary question was a matter for Congress ultimately to decide.

In the meantime, President Taylor died in office on July 9, 1850, and was succeeded by Vice President Millard Fillmore. Fillmore was a New Englander, who, as a member of Congress, opposed the annexation of Texas as a slave territory. Less cautious in his approach than his predecessor had been, he flatly denied that Texas had any claim to New Mexico whatsoever. Fillmore warned that his constitutional duty obligated him to act:

> If Texas militia, therefore, march into any one of the other states, or into any territory of the United States, to execute or enforce any law of Texas, they . . . are to be regarded merely as intruders; and if, within such state or territory they obstruct any law of the United States, either by power or arms, or mere power of numbers, or constitute such a combination as is too powerful to be suppressed by the civil authority, the President of the United States has no option left to him, but that of using force in carrying out the acts of Congress.[14]

---

13. Ibid., p. 142.
14. Beck, p. 143 (citing James D. Richardson, ed. *A Compilation of the Messages and Papers of the Presidents*, vol. 4, p. 2605).

As a further warning to Texas, 750 additional troops were sent into New Mexico. This brought an angry retort from Alexander H. Stevens, who declared in Congress that "the first federal gun that shall be fired against the people of Texas without the authority of the law will be a signal for the free man from the Delaware to the Rio Grande to rally to the rescue."[15] While most members of Congress sided with New Mexico against the Texas claim, the situation was so serious that an immediate resolution was needed. It came in the form of the Compromise of 1850, proposed by Senator James Alfred Pearce of Maryland.[16]

According to the Compromise of 1850, Mexico's eastern boundary line was fixed at 103 degrees west longitude.[17] In exchange for giving up its claims to eastern New Mexico, the United States paid Texas ten million dollars. The Compromise of 1850 did not grant statehood to New Mexico; Congress turned down this request chiefly because of the polarization of the slavery issue. The compromise instead divided the land gained from Mexico (exclusive of California) into two territories, the Utah Territory and the New Mexico Territory.

In 1861, New Mexico's northern border was redrawn. The discovery of gold in the Colorado Rockies in 1859 resulted in a rush to the area. The population grew rapidly, which led Congress to form the Colorado Territory in February 1861. By its action, Congress moved New Mexico's northern border southward to thirty-seven degrees north latitude. As a result, New Mexico lost its settlements in the San Luis Valley and along the Conejos River. It also lost control of the rich coal deposits near Trinidad.

GADSDEN PURCHASE OF 1853

Much of the new international boundary in western New Mexico (present-day Arizona) established by the Treaty of Guadalupe Hidalgo

---

15. Beck, p. 143 (quoting William Campbell Binkley, "The Question of Texan Jurisdiction in New Mexico under the United States, 1848–50," *Southwestern Historical Quarterly*, vol. 24 [July 1920], p. 37).
16. The compromise was a final effort to avoid war, but it only delayed the Civil War for ten years.
17. The line was, in fact, one-half mile west of this longitude.

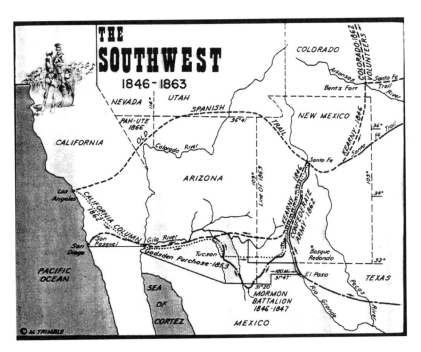

Map of the Southwest, 1846-1863. (MAP BY DEAN LYON, ART BY JACK GRAHAM, COURTESY OF MARSHALL TRIMBLE, DIRECTOR OF THE MARICOPA COMMUNITY COLLEGE SOUTHWEST STUDIES PROGRAM)

was north of the Gila River, leaving the route to California, constructed by the Mormon Battalion, running through Mexican territory. This leg of the route through Mexican territory, along with an international boundary dispute near El Paso, Texas, nearly led to another war between Mexico and the United States. Franklin Pierce, following his inauguration as the fourteenth president on March 4, 1853, sent James Gadsden to Mexico City with an offer to purchase additional territory from Mexico, which the United States believed it needed for a southern route to connect the lower Mississippi valley to California.

The first plan was to purchase all the land south of the Gila River in the western part of the territory and part, if not all, of Sonora in order to include the port of Guaymas on the Gulf of California, plus all of Baja California. The offered price of $20 million was attractive to a Mexico in dire need of cash. However, the project ran into trouble, not as had been expected with the Mexican authorities, but with Congress. Cognizant of the looming breach between North and South, senators and congressmen from Northern states were not willing to see huge territories such as Sonora and Baja California acquired by the federal government, believing that such acquisition favored an expanding Southern economy and the culture of slavery all the way to the Pacific Coast. Moreover, if a railroad was to reach the Pacific, the Northern adherents wanted it in Northern territory, west from Council Bluffs rather than west from New Orleans. The debate in Congress continued until an agreement was finally reached. The border was set where it is today, allowing ample room for a wagon road and a railroad to cross the territory south of the Gila to California. The price of $10 million was accepted by Mexico, and on December 30, 1853, the Gadsden Purchase became a reality. To the American public, it was a seemingly useless expenditure; the ever-ready critics derided Congress for being so dumb as to buy a worthless desert. The Gadsden Purchase was considered absurd by much of the press, which often referred to the purchased tract as "our national cactus garden" and "rattlesnake heaven."[18]

In 1854, the southern boundary of New Mexico was established at its present location. All of New Mexico south of the thirty-fourth

---

18. Edward Corle, *The Gila*, p. 182.

James Gadsden, U. S. Minister to Mexico who negotiated the Gadsden Treaty with Mexico. (COURTESY OF MARSHALL TRIMBLE, DIRECTOR OF THE MARICOPA COMMUNITY COLLEGE SOUTHWEST STUDIES PROGRAM)

parallel between Texas and California was now part of the United States of America and was known as the Territory of New Mexico. The new land acquired through the Gadsden Purchase in the southeastern part of the territory became part of Doña Ana County. In the southwest, the Gila Valley and virtually its entire watershed came under the Stars and Stripes. A route to the west was now assured, the boundary issue was settled, an immense area was now available for settling, and untold wealth in mineral rights lay ready for the grabbing. But the United States acquired something they had not bargained for—the hostile Apache Indians. And the most dramatic change to New Mexico's boundaries came in 1863, when the territory was divided in half and the western portion made a separate Arizona Territory.

CHAPTER NINE

Breaking New Ground: Territorial Years

Among the early arrivals were Yankees from New England, French-men from Louisiana, Germans leaving their European fatherland, and a sprinkling of Jews whose contribution to New Mexico's sanity has never been adequately celebrated.

—Erna Fergusson, *New Mexico: A Pageant of Three Peoples*

After the United States' acquisition of New Mexico, Anglo-Americans entering the state were small in number, but large in influence. Coming first in trickles, the new arrivals began to increase in numbers as word of free land and big opportunities got back to the eastern states and over the Atlantic to Europe. New England Yankees, Frenchmen from Louisiana, Germans, and a sprinkling of Jews found their way to New Mexico. Englishmen arrived seeking adventure, if that was their ambition, or investment if they were rich. Among the latter was Captain William French, Irish by birth but a "stiffly British officer to the backbone," whose *Recollections* recall wild days in the territory's southwestern corner in the years after the Civil War. He established his ranch on the San Francisco River.[1]

Many of the earlier arrivals wrote about what they saw as a strange land. Santa Fe, the most important town, was described as "having the appearance of an extensive brickyard or of looking like a group of flat boats clustered together at a river wharf." Taos, likewise, failed to impress the Americans who depicted it as a "collection of mud

---

1. Fergusson, *Three Peoples*, p. 282.

houses around a miserable square." Even the governor's palace, the most important building in the province, was seen only as "a mud building supported by rough pine pillars." But as historian Warren A. Beck wrote, these observers failed to grasp that in the New Mexico of the nineteenth century, some of the Middle Ages had been preserved, and, he adds, it was a land where time had almost stood still, where much that was common in sixteenth-century Spain still existed.[2]

Much of this new land acquired from Mexico was unknown to Anglo-Americans, apart from a few fearless mountain men, who had earlier traversed the area's mountains and deserts in search of furs. Consequently, one of the first undertakings for the United States government was to survey and map routes for transporting passengers and freight. This responsibility was assigned to the Army Corps of Topographical Engineers, a specialized cadre of audacious explorer-scientists. The first of these daring explorers was Captain Lorenzo Sitgreaves, who led a survey party along the thirty-fifth parallel in 1851. Two years later, Lieutenant A. W. Wipple led a small survey party westward from Zuni to Cajon Pass, California. There were other expeditions, as exploration of the vast new territory continued through the 1850s.[3]

Travel within New Mexico prior to the area's acquisition from Mexico had been essentially in the north-south direction, the merchants of Chihuahua transporting goods to be bartered in Santa Fe and Taos, then returning with the raw materials of the province. Following the territory's acquisition, east-west routes opened up, and overland travel through New Mexico to California increased steadily. Stagecoaches began arriving in 1857, with the opening of the San Antonio–San Diego Mail Line. Dubbed the "Jackass Mail," its passengers had to exchange their coach seats for a saddle mule over part of the desert journey.

The following year, the leather-slung coaches of John Butterfield's Overland Mail began a spectacular twenty-six-day run from St. Louis

---

2. Beck, pp. 200–201.
3. The contribution of the Mormon Battalion in this regard cannot be overlooked. The battalion led by Philip St. George Cooke arrived in Santa Fe from Fort Leavenworth in October 1846, then marched along the Rio Grande and west across Arizona to San Diego, where it arrived on January 29, 1847. "Cooke's Wagon Road," as it was called, became the potential route for railroad construction.

through New Mexico to San Francisco. Thoroughly reliable, it was shut down only once in its thirty-month history, when Cochise and his Chiricahua Apaches went on the warpath near Apache Pass. After the Civil War, trade on the Santa Fe Trail continued to flourish until the late 1870s, when the railroads invaded New Mexico and "the picturesque Santa Fe trade was over."[4] During the 1850s, numerous military posts, extending from Fort Union north of Las Vegas to Fort Fillmore near Mesilla in southern New Mexico, were erected to check the Indian tribes that continued to raid throughout the territory. The presence of the military encouraged expansion of settlements along the frontier in areas along the Upper Chama Valley, in southern Colorado's San Luis Valley, and in other regions in central and southern New Mexico. Between 1850 and 1860, New Mexico's population grew from sixty-one thousand to ninety-three thousand.[5]

While New Mexico adjusted to its new place in the Union, its predominant Catholic population was adapting to ecclesiastical administrative changes.[6] Soon after New Mexico was ceded to the United States, the American Catholic leaders meeting in Baltimore in 1848 petitioned the Holy See to let the ecclesiastical administration of the Mexican territory east of California come under its jurisdiction. Responsibility for church affairs had rested with the bishop of Durango during the Mexican period. A French clergyman, Jean Baptiste Lamy, who had already had a great deal of experience in America as a priest in Ohio, was consecrated as the first bishop of the newly established diocese in 1853. Much has been written about this man, who, according to one historian, "possessed an unflagging store of energy that made it possible for him to impart to his diocesan duties a zeal which insured success."[7] He labored tirelessly among Anglos, Mexicans, and Indians to bring reform to a religious community that had been allowed to grow stagnant and corrupt under some twenty years of Mexican rule.

---

4.   Beck, p. 118.
5.   Roberts, p. 216.
6.   Catholicism was practically the only religion in the territory; Protestant clergy made efforts to set up churches only after the railroads came and brought Anglo settlers in large numbers.
7.   Beck, p. 214.

Bishop Jean Baptiste Lamy, c. 1860s.

EXPLORING NEW MARKETS: JEWISH MERCHANT AND TRADER

General Kearney's conquest of New Mexico opened the way for an array of adventurers and entrepreneurs to seek their fortunes in the newly acquired territory, letting them share in its opportunities and trade in ways and on a scale unknown in the territory before then.

These adventurers and entrepreneurs came from both north and south, bringing with them their sectional lifestyles and prejudices. Those who came along the Santa Fe Trail were, as one writer put it, "best fitted to adjust to New Mexico's unique patterns because many of them were Europeans who spoke at least two languages and readily learned another."[8] Chief among them were Jewish immigrants who began arriving in the 1840s. Their successes and fortunes were realized within the framework of a new and changing economic order, which William Parish, a leading scholar of business history in New Mexico, credits them for setting in motion. Moving into the most remote, as well as the most populous, areas, these Jewish immigrants used every opportunity to establish their position as traders and, as a result, helped draw New Mexico into the mainstream of America's commercial life and out of the relative isolation in which it had previously existed.[9] In the words of Professor Henry J. Tobias: "They bought from New Mexican farmers for the army and for the Indians, they also bought in the East for all their customers. They sold commodities purchased in the East to the local population and had to supply credit for their local producers to produce and buy."[10] They became wholesalers and retailers, and the extent of their operations carried them far beyond the limits of Santa Fe and Albuquerque into the vast territory beyond. Families named Spiegelberg, Zeckendorf, Lesinsky, Traurer, Staab, and Leitensdorfer, to mention a few, were among the movers and shakers of nineteenth-century New Mexico trade and commerce.

---

8. Fergusson, *Three Peoples,* pp. 281–282.
9. Tobias, *The History of the Jews in New Mexico,* p. 65.
10. Ibid., p. 65.

Temple Montitore, Las Vegas, NM, erected 1885.

Spiegelberg Block, St. Francisco Street at Plaza, Santa Fe, NM, c. 1896.

The relative openness of Western society at the time facilitated a climate of goodwill between Jew and Christian, which made it easier for the immigrant Jew to function. Nowhere was this goodwill more profound than in the personal relationship between the Spiegelberg family and Archbishop John Lamy of Santa Fe. It was a friendship that began in 1852, when the newly appointed bishop, en route to Santa Fe, tended to the dysentery-stricken Levi Spiegelberg on the Santa Fe Trail.[11] The friendship received public manifestation when the Spiegelbergs (as well as the Staabs) contributed large sums toward the construction of Santa Fe's St. Francis Cathedral in 1869. In consideration for the Jewish support, Lamy had engraved in the keystone of the arch of the main entrance the Hebrew letters for Yahweh.[12] Were there Jewish merchants in New Mexico before the American period? The general conditions of settlement would not have favored their entry. Before they could appear in New Mexico, Jews would have had to be present in New Spain, where circumstances favored only Catholics. That crypto-Jews[13] lived in New Mexico seems beyond dispute.[14]

Gathering Clouds of Civil War

New Mexico played a small but significant role in the Civil War. In July 1861, Confederate forces from Texas captured the southern New Mexico settlement of Mesilla and, early the following year, launched an attack on Fort Craig, south of Socorro. Their plan was to capture critical supplies at the fort, then move north to take Albuquerque, Santa Fe, and, most important, the military supply depot at Fort Union. However, the Union cause ultimately prevailed in thwarting a Confederacy takeover of New Mexico.

---

11. Ibid., p. 79 (citing Floyd S. Fierman, "The Triangle and the Tetragrammaton: A Note on the Cathedral at Santa Fe," *NMHR* 37, no. 4 [October 1962], pp. 313–314; Flora Spiegelberg, "Tribute to Archbishop Lamy of New Mexico," *El Palacio* 36, no. 3–4 [January 1934], pp. 23–24).
12. Ibid., p. 80.
13. *Crypto* means "secret" here.
14. Tobias, p. 11 (citing Martin A. Cohen, "Some Misconceptions about the Crypto-Jews in Colonial Mexico," *American Jewish Historical Quarterly* 61, no. 4 [1972], pp. 280–281).

With the exception of the residents in the southeastern and south-western regions of the territory, most New Mexicans remained loyal to the Union cause, and many of them performed willingly as militia or scouts for the regular army.[15] Defection to the Confederate side in the southeast occurred in the area of Mesilla, where most of the inhabitants were Texans who had moved there after the Gadsden Purchase. Feeling neglected by the government in Santa Fe, they had made several unsuccessful petitions in the 1850s, calling on Congress to establish a separate territory. When Texas seceded from the Union after the outbreak of the Civil War, they organized a convention in March 1861 and announced themselves as the Territory of Arizona[16] (which included all the lands below the thirty-fourth parallel between Texas and California). Forming a government, they petitioned for admission to the Confederacy as a territory. Some three hundred miles to the west, the residents of Tucson warmly greeted Captain Sherod Hunter and his fifty-four mounted riflemen when they arrived in February 1862 and raised the Confederate flag over the old pueblo. At the time, the defection of Tucson, with its small population, was not regarded as serious, but the defection of Mesilla in close proximity to Fort Fillmore was another matter.

At the outbreak of the war, federal forces were operating a number of small forts throughout the territory, primarily as a means of defense against the ever-present hostile Indians. Along the Rio Grande were Fort Craig, Fort Fillmore, and Fort Bliss near El Paso. East of the Rio Grande were Fort Union near Las Vegas, Fort Marcy at Santa Fe, and Fort Stanton in the Lincoln Mountains. In the west were Fort Defiance near the present Arizona state line and Fort Breckenridge and Fort Buchanan near Tucson. As these scattered forts depended on supplies from Fort Leavenworth, getting the supplies was a critical problem after the Civil War broke out. More serious than the problem of supplies, however, was the problem of military morale. As their home states seceded, officer after officer had to decide where his loyalties

---

15. Beck, p. 147.
16. Originally a Spanish term for the site of a silver discovery near present-day Nogales, Mexico, the name *Arizona* was derived from a Tohono O'odham (Papago Indian) word, *arizonac*, meaning "little spring."

lay. Many resigned their New Mexico assignments and reenlisted in the Confederate Army.[17]

Confederates Invade New Mexico

The first invasion of New Mexico by Confederate forces occurred on July 23, 1861, when Captain John Robert Baylor arrived at Mesilla with a force of 258 Texas cavalrymen and occupied the village without firing a shot. Two days later, a party of Union troops from Fort Fillmore marched on Mesilla and confronted the Confederates. After a brief encounter in which three Union soldiers were killed and six were wounded, the Union side withdrew. Captain Baylor then read a proclamation claiming all of New Mexico south of the thirty-fourth parallel for the Confederate States of America. He named it the Territory of Arizona, designated Mesilla as the seat of the territorial government, and appointed himself as governor.[18] With the subsequent capture of Fort Fillmore, the Territory of Arizona was solidly annexed to the Confederate States of America.

In December 1861, Brigadier General Henry Hopkins Sibley (formerly a major in the United States Army) set out from Fort Bliss to capture all of New Mexico for the Confederacy. The first encounter was at Val Verde (near Fort Craig) on February 12, 1862. Sibley's army of 2,600 men engaged a force of 3,800 Union regulars and volunteers led by Colonel Edward Canby. Historians chalk it up as a defeat for the Union side that suffered 306 casualties; Confederate casualties were 185.

With the way clear, the Confederates headed for Albuquerque, meeting little resistance as they moved up the Rio Grande valley. After a brief engagement with the bluecoats, Sibley captured Albuquerque on March 2 and raised the Confederate flag in the plaza. He then ordered the Union quartermaster to destroy what supplies he could not take with him. They pressed on to Santa Fe, New Mexico's capital, where Sibley discovered that the capital had been vacated and most of

---

17. Beck, p. 149 (citing William A. Keleher, *Turmoil in New Mexico*, p. 191).
18. Josephy, *The Civil War in the American West*, p. 40.

the supplies had been hauled to the safety of Fort Union. In addition, the territorial government, including Governor Henry Connelly, had fled to the safety of the fort. Sibley took Santa Fe without firing a shot, and the flag of the Confederacy was raised over the old adobe Palace of the Governors.

The Confederates advanced toward Fort Union next but never reached there. Instead, they encountered Union forces at Apache Canyon on the west side of Glorieta Pass, where the pivotal battle of the Civil War in New Mexico began on March 26, 1862; Union troops from Fort Union, volunteers from Colorado, and the New Mexico militia confronted the Confederate army. They vied for control of this strategic pass for three days, until a Union raiding party penetrated the rear of the Confederate positions and destroyed their supply train. Desperately short of supplies, the Confederates were forced to retreat.

CONFEDERATES ROUTED

Confederate forces suffered a major defeat at Glorieta Pass; 350 men were lost, while Union losses numbered 150. Although little noted among the greater battles of the eastern war zone, this skirmish was a decisive one, for it ended the Confederacy's plans for New Mexico and held the Southwest for the Union.[19] If the Confederacy had held onto New Mexico, it would have succeeded in securing that much-needed passage to California.

Some historians call Glorieta Pass the "Gettysburg of the West." For New Mexicans it was more than a Civil War battle victory, it was their victory over the Texans. Erna Fergusson writes: "Old people, in my own youth, used to recount what they remembered of the terrible *Tejanos*.[20] Huge men they were, red and hairy, uttering incomprehensible noises instead of words, frightening babies, stealing cattle . . . and, when drunk, even desecrating chapels."[21] Sibley left Santa Fe on

---

19. Fergusson, *Our Southwest,* p. 272.
20. To average Mexicans, *tejano* meant a person who was loathed and hated.
21. Fergusson, *Three Peoples,* p. 272.

April 8 and retreated down the valley. Major Jose Sena with a New
Mexico volunteer company gave Sibley a final trouncing at Peralta
near Albuquerque. About the same time, a two-thousand-man force
led by Colonel James H. Carleton was heading east from California.
Arriving at Tucson in May 1862, Carleton found that the Confederates, who had held the pueblo for three months, had already withdrawn. He proclaimed martial law, made himself military governor,
and reestablished Union authority. Two weeks later he headed east,
arriving on July 4 at the Rio Grande near Fort Thorn. By then, Sibley
and most of the units that had made up the Army of New Mexico had
abandoned the territory and were retreating across the searing plains
of West Texas. With them went the last of the prominent civilian seces-
sionists in the area, thus ending one phase of New Mexico's history.

New Mexico Partitioned

It became evident shortly after the signing of the Gadsden Purchase
Treaty that the Territory of New Mexico was too large and unmanage-
able to be efficiently administered and that a breakup was necessary.
Tucson, the largest city in the Gadsden Purchase area, was 250 miles
from the county seat at Mesilla, and more than 500 miles by stage
from Santa Fe, the territorial capital. Hence the citizens of the Santa
Cruz Valley, for the most part, made and administered their own laws.

As early as 1856, Congress had been petitioned to set up a separate territory for Arizona, and several bills introduced toward this end
had failed passage. Most of the early plans suggested for an "Arizona
Territory" would have embraced only the southern parts of present-
day Arizona and New Mexico. Hoping to goad Congress into speedier
action, a provisional government was formed at a Tucson convention
in April 1860. Delegates drew up a constitution that they believed
would accommodate the area until the federal government created
an official Arizona Territory. However, the pre–Civil War struggle
over slavery precluded the formation of any new political units, and
the question of the separation of New Mexico into two territories lay
dormant until the Republican Party gained control of Congress. The

creation of new territories and states, likely to be loyal to the Union, then emerged as part of the new administration's overall strategy. Interestingly, it was the Civil War, in a secondary way, that aided Arizona's separate-territory cause by bringing about rivalry for control of the Southwest. The newly established Confederate government in Richmond provoked Washington action by crafting its own blueprint for an "Arizona Territory"—one that comprised the southern segment of New Mexico between Texas and California. Faced with this threat to the Union, Congress passed the Organic Act in 1863 creating the Territory of Arizona from the western portion of New Mexico. John N. Goodwin of Maine was appointed governor, and when he got to Santa Fe, General Carleton advised him to stay away from Tucson and head instead straight into the wilderness and establish his capital well to the north of both Mexicans and Southern sympathizers. Following Carleton's advice, the Yankee governor headed west until he came across an idyllic spot in the wilderness near the present railroad station of Navajo Springs, and there on December 29, 1863, he established the capital of the newly formed territory and called it Prescott.[22]

---

22. Ibid., pp. 174–175.

CHAPTER TEN

Indian Wars and Relocation of Indians to Reservations

The program he [Brigadier General Carleton] presented to Governor Connelly, Chief Justice Kirby Benedict, and other territorial officials was direct and harsh: wage merciless war against all hostile tribes, force them to their knees, and then confine them to reservations.

—Marc Simmons, *New Mexico: An Interpretive History*

When the United States took over the government at Santa Fe in 1846, it acquired not only the vast Indian-inhabited territory, which included present-day New Mexico, but also the responsibility for making peace with the native populations of the area, of whom the Athabaskan-speaking people, differentiated by this time as Navajo and Apache, were foremost. This was to prove far more difficult than anyone could have realized at the time, and it resulted in almost forty years of difficult and costly fighting with much destruction and bloodshed on both sides.

NAVAJO CAMPAIGN

For more than three hundred years, the Navajos battled their traditional enemies—the Comanche and the Utes. They fought a long series of raid and counter-raid wars with the Spanish and later with the Mexicans. In the 1770s, the Spaniards managed to restrain them, after which they experienced a long and bitter period of slave trading and territorial encroachment. In the twenty years after 1800, the Navajos embarked on raiding on a big scale. They made war on the Spaniards at Canyon de Chelly in 1804 but suffered a bloody defeat. In 1821, during a truce conference with a Spanish commander, twenty-four of their warriors were treacherously murdered, "each stabbed in the heart as he smoked in peace and hope."[1]

Navajo tribes ran wild in northeastern New Mexico throughout the 1820s, especially after Mexican independence in 1824. In fact, Navajo raiding had become such a menace that when General Kearney set up headquarters at Santa Fe, he found the various Pueblos from Taos to Zuni, as well as the Mexican population of northwestern New Mexico, willing to ally themselves with American forces for a war against the predatory tribes. For a time, nothing was done to bring them to submission. Believing that peace treaties were the answer, Kearney sent Colonel Alexander William Doniphan with a company of Missouri volunteers into Navajo country to parley with them. Believing that he was negotiating with a united tribe, Doniphan proceeded to work out a peace treaty with the headmen of bands living to the north of Bear Springs. As it turned out, these headmen had little authority, and, as a result, the treaty had little value. Various Navajo bands continued to raid in precisely the same way as before.[2]

After numerous unsuccessful attempts to deal with the Navajos, it became apparent to the federal government that the problem of Navajo raids could not be settled with treaties and that a decisive military campaign would have to be undertaken. This led to the establishment of a military post, Fort Defiance, in the heart of Navajo country. The Navajos looked at this as an invasion of their homeland and organized a force of two thousand warriors (armed with mostly bows and arrows) in 1860, in an attempt to drive the military from Fort Defiance. After a two-hour battle and with many of their numbers killed or wounded, the Indians retreated. Although the Navajos failed in this attempt, it did not deter them from continuing to raid, which was undertaken with more intensity in many neighborhoods.[3]

---

1. Fergusson, *Three Peoples,* p. 82.
2. Spicer, p. 216.
3. Ibid.

Navajo Hogan at Crystal, NM, 1929. (PHOTO BY WILLIAM R. SASSAMAN)

Navajo Hogan, summer shelter and flock of sheep (1940).

When troops were withdrawn for the Civil War effort in 1861, Fort Defiance, along with other forts, was abandoned. The two-year absence of the military that followed had the Navajos believing they had succeeded in ousting the Americans. However, as Union troops regained control of the Rio Grande valley from the Confederates, a determined effort was launched to destroy, at all costs, the Navajo threat in the territory. Brigadier General James H. Carleton, the newly appointed military commander of New Mexico, issued an order declaring all-out war on the Navajos in 1862. He selected Colonel Christopher (Kit) Carson for the job, instructing him to round up all Navajos, peacefully if possible, and move them to the Bosque Redondo near Fort Sumner. The Navajos refused to move.[4]

Carson moved swiftly and, with seven hundred volunteers, marched into the heart of Navajo country and began a systematic campaign of destroying all Navajo means of livelihood. His soldiers scorched cornfields and slaughtered livestock by the thousands. There were no major battles, but Carson's military operation left the Navajo economy in ruins. Navajos began to scatter to find food, some to southern New Mexico and southern Arizona, some westward to Navajo Mountain, and some to join the Apaches in White Mountain; many women went to Jemez pueblo. By the end of 1863, some were even showing up at Fort Defiance to surrender. Carson persisted in his pursuit and, early in 1864, led his troops into Canyon de Chelly, where they encountered a large number of Navajo. Marching through the canyon, he renewed his campaign of destroying all Navajo means of livelihood. Exhausted, starving, and faced with annihilation, the Navajos capitulated. After Canyon de Chelly, some eight thousand Navajos were rounded up by the legendary mountain-man-turned-soldier, who herded them like cattle on the infamous three-hundred-mile walk from Canyon de Chelly to Bosque Redondo, where they were placed on a government reservation.[5]

---

4.   Ibid., p. 218.
5.   Fergusson, *Three Peoples*, p. 86.

BOSQUE REDONDO

At Bosque Redondo the Navajos were confined within Fort Sumner, joining some four hundred Mescalero Apaches already there. For four years they were crammed together in a solitary, closely supervised, and closely regulated group. Their way of life was completely altered, from roving herders to sedentary prisoners. Disease and confinement reduced their numbers. In 1865, a smallpox epidemic killed 2,300 people within a few months. The tribe made one dash for freedom, but was rounded up by Apache scouts (a newly formed arm of the military) and returned to the reservation.[6]

As the situation worsened, it became evident to the War Department that General Carleton's relocation program was not working. Following an investigation by General Sherman, the decision was made to allow the Navajos to return to their homeland, subject, of course, to their leaders signing a ten-year treaty agreeing to government terms. In 1868, their chiefs signed a treaty agreeing to keep the peace; in exchange, the U.S. government agreed to restore them to their ancient homeland in the Four Corners area. To help them restart their livelihoods, the government distributed fourteen thousand sheep and one thousand goats to the ninety-five hundred Navajos who showed up at the distribution center.[7] The Navajos were on the road to a new livelihood as independent herdsmen, and, from it, the blueprint of modern Navajo life emerged.

APACHE MENACE

Throughout the Spanish period, the Apaches, like the Navajos, remained on the periphery of the Spanish administrative-missionary system. Their territory never became the setting of actual Spanish settlements. Notwithstanding, there was contact, first through mutual raiding and active hostilities and then through acquaintance with Spanish material

---

6.   Ibid.
7.   Ibid., p. 220.

culture. For example, the use of horses and better war accoutrements were aspects of material culture gained from the Spaniards.[8]

Apaches chose warfare as a way of life and, over a period of 150 years, made it an integral part of their culture. Historian Edward Spicer maintains that this choice of warfare, encouraged by contact with the Spaniards, aroused the Apaches to rebellion.[9] As their hostilities and raiding intensified during the early 1700s, so did their control of a 250-mile-wide stretch of territory separating New Mexico from Sonora-Chihuahua. This was an area where there were no Spanish settlements and no manifestation of Spanish control. It was also the area where Apache culture matured during the next century and where Anglo-Americans first came into contact with them in the nineteenth century.[10]

In an effort to control the Apaches, the states of Chihuahua and Sonora offered bounties on Apache scalps. Some Anglo-Americans entered into this trade along with the Mexicans. The immediate result, during the 1830s, was a fierce outbreak of Apache fighting.[11] In an infamous incident in 1837, in an effort to acquire scalps, a character named Johnson fired a howitzer into a group near Janos, killing several peaceful Mimbreno Apaches and their influential leader, Juan José. This action turned Mangas Coloradas, the legendary Apache chieftain and a relative of Juan José, into an enemy of the white men. Under his leadership, the Mimbreno Apaches forced the closure of the Santa Rita mines and drove the Mexicans from southwest New Mexico.

Following the acquisition of New Mexico by the United States, Apache leaders found themselves faced with a policy that they would not accept. Under the pacification provision of the Treaty of Guadalupe Hidalgo, requiring them to make treaties with the Anglo-Americans, they were prohibited from conducting raids on Mexican territory. To the Apaches, this was an unreasonable position, Anglo-Americans claiming, by virtue of having conquered the Mexicans, that they had become titleholder of Apache territory. As far as the Apaches

---

8.   Spicer, p. 241.
9.   Ibid., p. 243.
10. Ibid., p. 236.
11. Ibid., p. 245.

Mangas, son of Mangas Colorado, the legendary Apache Chieftain who died in 1863.
(COURTESY OF MARSHALL TRIMBLE, DIRECTOR OF THE MARICOPA COMMUNITY COLLEGE SOUTHWEST STUDIES PROGRAM)

were concerned, the Mexicans had never conquered them, so, for that reason, how could the Anglo-Americans, as a result of conquering the Mexicans, lay claim to Apache land?[12]

With pressure on the military to keep the east-west routes open at all costs following recovery of New Mexico from the Confederates, General Carleton, from his headquarters in Santa Fe, declared a war of extermination against the Apaches. He was determined to keep the coalition of Mimbrenos and Chiricahuas, led by Chiefs Mangas Coloradas and Cochise, under control in order to keep the Overland Mail running. He established Fort Bowie inside Chiricahua territory and increased troops at Fort Webster. Within a few months after reoccupying Fort Webster, Mangas Coloradas was killed in a skirmish. Cochise died in 1874, and the Chiricahua command selected an Apache named Geronimo as their war leader. Geronimo, who grew up in eastern Arizona, had followed the great chief Mangas Coloradas to Mexico in 1850. He hated Mexicans because they had killed his mother, wife, and three children. The Chiricahuas, led by Geronimo, continued to raid into Mexico, and they harassed the Americans wherever they ran up against them in New Mexico and southern Arizona.

Anglo-American intrusion onto Apache territory continued in the form of miners, farmers, and ranchers. Apaches were willing to allow settlement of their territory by incoming Americans, provided the settlers paid them for the privilege of mining or ranching. Some American ranchers were already doing this, when an event occurred in 1861 that abruptly disturbed the friendly and sincere relationships that had developed through a mutual understanding between Indian and settler. The event, known as the Bascom Affair, was a blunder by the military that touched off what would become a long and ruthless war between the military and the Apaches. It began when Lieutenant George Nicholas Bascom, a young cavalry officer stationed in Chiricahua territory, sought to recover a Mexican captive from the Chiricahuas by taking their leader, Cochise, and some warriors as hostages during peace talks. Cochise escaped, and Bascom murdered the other hostages. Cochise retaliated by murdering an American trader and

---

12. Ibid., p. 245–246.

Geronimo, the legendary Chiricahua Apache warrior. (COURTESY OF MARSHALL TRIMBLE, DIRECTOR OF THE MARICOPA COMMUNITY COLLEGE SOUTHWEST STUDIES PROGRAM)

the cycle of assault and reprisal escalated.[13] A few days later, Cochise burned a wagon train, killing nine Mexicans and taking four Americans prisoners. The bloody spiral accelerated as he attacked Bascom's command next, albeit unsuccessfully. Cochise then executed the four American prisoners he was holding hostage. Bascom's men hung six Apache warriors in retaliation, including Cochise's brother and two nephews. From the Bascom incident, a bloody, treacherous war evolved between the American military and the Chiricahua Apaches. Many lives were lost, much property was destroyed, and intense suffering was inflicted on the lives of many innocent families.

ROUNDUP OF APACHES

In 1876, federal authorities rounded up several bands of Apaches, including Geronimo and his warriors, and placed them on a reservation at San Carlos. It was described as "Hell's Forty Acres." The move proved unwise. The restive Apaches, especially the Chiricahua, abhorred reservation living, and, to make matters worse, conditions on the reservation were appalling. After rumors that all Apaches would be moved to Oklahoma, it was only a matter of time before some incident or other would spark a riot. It came when the agency's chief of police tried to arrest an Indian. The suspect ran and the officer fired into a crowd of people, killing a woman. The Chiricahua screamed for justice. When it was not forthcoming, they waited for the opportune moment and then seized the police chief and beheaded him. Afterward, Geronimo and several hundred of his people bolted the reservation and fled into Mexico's Sierra Madre Mountains, where he resumed a life of raiding in the border areas of Mexico and the United States.

General George Crook was recalled in 1882 to pursue Geronimo. During an earlier campaign in Arizona's central mountains, Crook had subdued the Yavapai and Tonto Apaches in a matter of months. He began his campaign into the Sierra Madre Mountains in 1883, after receiving permission from the Republic of Mexico to cross the

13. Ibid., p. 247.

border. His army penetrated into the Indians' "natural fortress" in the Sierra Madre, dealing the Chiricahua a psychological defeat. Crook's destroy-and-burn strategy forced the Chiricahua to negotiate. Crook's terms were precise: return to the reservation at once. They agreed, and within a few months Geronimo and his people were back in San Carlos. It was only a matter of time until Geronimo and his followers bolted from the reservation again and, once again, Crook's men pursued them into the Sierra Madre Mountains. A meeting took place at Canyon de los Embudos on March 25, 1886. Geronimo surrendered to Crook and agreed to his terms: two years exile for Geronimo and his band in Florida before being allowed to return to the reservation in San Carlos. However, the wily chief gave several lectures on the injustices that his people had suffered at the hands of the white man, before agreeing to the terms. Crook then headed back to his headquarters at Fort Bowie to wire the news to Washington, and the Indians started their journey back to the United States. At one of the stops along the way, a whiskey peddler managed to gain access to Geronimo's camp. After getting the warrior and some of his followers intoxicated, the peddler informed Geronimo that General Cook's men were planning to kill him. The next morning Geronimo and some of his followers were missing.[14] When word reached Washington of Geronimo's escape, Crook was replaced by General Nelson Miles. Miles sent a trusted officer, Lieutenant Charles B. Gatewood, to seek Geronimo's surrender and agreement to the previous terms. Exhausted and hopelessly outnumbered, Geronimo had little choice. He agreed but insisted on surrendering to General Miles personally; the historic surrender took place at Skeleton Canyon, a few miles southeast of Geronimo Mountain, on September 4, 1886. Geronimo and his Chiricahua followers were held at Fort Bowie for a few days and then loaded on wagons and hauled a few miles north to the railroad at Bowie station, from where they were shipped to a prison camp in Florida, where they spent not the agreed upon two years, but a full ten. Despite captivity, Geronimo rode in President Theodore Roosevelt's inaugural parade in 1905. He died in Oklahoma in 1909, without ever again setting foot in his native Apacheria, where bitter

---

14. Trimble, *Roadside History of Arizona*, p. 82–83.

General George Crook. (COURTESY OF MARSHALL TRIMBLE,
DIRECTOR OF THE MARICOPA COMMUNITY COLLEGE
SOUTHWEST STUDIES PROGRAM)

memories of the Apache wars endured in the minds of the people—Anglo, Mexican, and Indian—for several generations. They buried him in the Apache cemetery at Fort Sill.

CONQUEST OF APACHERIA

In the land called Apacheria, which straddled the boundary of New Mexico and Arizona, the Apaches maintained the upper hand for centuries—first in their wars with the Spaniards and later with the Mexicans. But it would take the tenacity of the Americans to make the final conquest of the region possible, and it would take many years of tough guerrilla warfare to accomplish the feat. Historian Dan F. Trapp describes it more aptly than most:

> The conquest of Apacheria, stained with the blood of thousands, and washed in the heroism and valor of men of different races, is an American saga and one that needs to be told. Through it was seized the last great block of continent to be made part of the American commonwealth. Through it was resolved for all time the question of supremacy between aborigine and settler, white man and red. Through it was perpetuated grief and terror and bloody-handed savagery and nobleness until the inevitable was brought about, until the land was lost and made secure for the whites.[15]

---

15. Thrapp, *Conquest of Apacheria.* p. 5.

CHAPTER ELEVEN

Growth and Progress in the Territorial Years

There is not a single navigable stream to be found in New Mexico. The famous Rio del Norte is so shallow that, for the most part of the year, Indian canoes can scarcely float in it.

—Josiah Gregg, *The Commerce of the Prairies*

Throughout the territorial years, many hardy individuals braved the unkind elements to put up with the harsh realities of New Mexico's frontier environment. They were miners, farmers, ranchers, soldiers, and a slew of others, but it was the burro prospector, above all, who unchained the wilderness for others to follow. Attracted by the lure of gold and silver, he and his fuzzy-faced companion combed the mountains and the ravines in search of the treasure that had eluded Coronado and other explorers. Much has been penned about the prospector himself, but few have sung the praises of the fuzzy-faced burro. Erna Fergusson wrote "Southwestern civilization rode a long time burro-back. Where horses cannot go, a burro can. In long patient files he hauled . . .

ore from the Santa Rita mines down to Chihuahua; he grunted under casks and chests all the way from Mexico to Santa Fe; trappers and prospectors packed the little beast with water-kegs, supplies of bacon and beans. Yes, around mines and haciendas the burro has moved the creaking crusher wheel, worked the pump, carried supplies in and ore out.[1]

---

1.   Fergusson, *Our Southwest,* p. 173.

Burro wagon on the Plaza at Santa Fe, NM, 1912. (PHOTO BY JESSE L. NUSBAUM)

ECONOMIC HISTORY

Until the middle of the twentieth century, the economic history of New Mexico was chiefly about farming and the raising of sheep and cattle. Before the Spaniards arrived, the Pueblo Indians had been working the soil for generations, and the early Spanish colonists had little choice but to become farmers and stock raisers to survive in the new land. Until the advent of the cattlemen after the Civil War, sheep dominated the territory's agricultural economy. The first permanent settlers arriving with Governor Oñate in 1598 found that sheep adapted well in the area's semiarid climate. Two hundred and fifty years later, Josiah Gregg wrote about the scale of sheep raising in New Mexico: as many as five hundred thousand were exported in a given year, and it was not uncommon for two hundred thousand to be driven to market in the mining centers of Mexico.[2] Mexicans were

---

2.   Gregg, *Commerce*, p. 134.

sheep men and remained so after they became American citizens. The California gold rush opened a new market, and taking mutton there on the hoof was a lucrative business. In 1849, Don Antonio José Luna drove ten thousand head of sheep to California and thereafter he and his partners, the Oteros, made the journey regularly.[3]

By the late 1860s, New Mexico's Anglo population had increased above the twelve thousand mark, and new settlements were springing up in many parts of the territory. Ironically, as the population was growing, the market for mutton was declining, mainly because the Anglo population, as well as the army troops in the West, refused to eat mutton. Beef was the preferred choice, and it was becoming more plentiful with the arrival of the longhorn herds from Texas.

The Anglos' aversion to mutton might very well have sounded the death knell for the sheep-raising industry, except that the demand for wool came to the rescue. Wool became a steady income-producing commodity with the arrival of the Boston buyers in New Mexico in the 1880s. Demand for the product pushed its annual yield to more than four million pounds within a short period. This trade made Las Vegas one of the nation's most important wool centers, where, according to one observer, "loaded wool wagons would back up four or five miles waiting to reach the crowded plaza, where bidding was conducted by the lifting of a finger."[4] This steady market generated an incentive to find ways to improve the yield of wool. The old *churros*, descendents of the Spanish *merinos*, were yielding only two or three pounds of wool, until they were bred with the *rambouillet* breed from Utah and Idaho. The result was an increase to an average of seven to eight pounds per sheep. After the U.S. Army subdued the Plains Indians, the sheep lands spread into eastern New Mexico, southern Colorado, and even the Texas Panhandle. Some sheep men owned thousands of acres, much of it land granted to their ancestors from the Spanish Crown or Mexican governors. Don Hilario Gonzales of San Hilario on the Canadian River was known as the richest sheep rancher in the 1870s and was said to have "run sheep on a thousand hills." Francisco Lopez ran another vast sheep empire ten miles

3.   Fergusson, *Our Southwest*, p. 316.
4.   Ibid., p. 321.

from San Hilario at San Lorenzo. Still others on the eastern plains had flocks that numbered in the thousands.[5] By the late 1880s, the sheep industry had entered a period of decline, and by the end of the century it had lost its position of economic dominance to that of cattle. In the pre-railroad era, sheep ranchers had maintained the advantage, as sheep were more easily trailed to distant markets than were cattle. The arrival of the railroad in New Mexico changed this. There was no longer a need to trail either cattle or sheep long distances. Efforts, albeit unsuccessful, were undertaken to buttress the decline in the market; by the mid-twentieth century, however, the halcyon days of the New Mexico sheep man had passed.

CATTLE BARONS

"The hated Texans brought the cattle industry to New Mexico, and in this case their invasion of the state was successful," wrote Warren Beck.[6] As far as is known, the first cattle imported to the New World consisted of a few Andalusian heifers and a young bull brought to Mexico in 1521 by Gregorio de Villalobos. He acquired them from the island of Santo Domingo in the West Indies, where they had been bred from the original herds.

Governor Oñate introduced cattle and sheep into New Mexico in 1598, but they did not assume a significant commercial role until after the Civil War. When the war was over, Texans found themselves with millions of longhorns roaming the vast southern Texas countryside, while states north of the Mason-Dixon Line were in demand of prime cattle to replenish stocks used up during the war. The result was a succession of cattle drives from Texas to the railheads in Kansas. One Texan, Charles Goodnight, believing that a more lucrative market existed to the west, drove his herds into the mining camps of northern New Mexico and Colorado. Combining his herd with that of Oliver Loving, later his partner, Goodnight left from a point west of Fort Worth, Texas, in June 1866. The two followed a trail that led

---

5.   Roberts, pp. 255–256.
6.   Beck, p. 258.

them from Fort Bellnap on the Brazos River to the Pecos at Horsehead Crossing, which they then followed northward to Hope's Crossing, where they entered New Mexico.[7] Goodnight and Loving found not only a lucrative market in the mining camps but also markets at the military forts scattered throughout the New Mexico territory. In addition to the needs of the soldiers, the government had to feed several thousand Indians who were penned up on the Bosque Redondo Reservation near Fort Sumner. While Goodnight hurried back to Texas for more cattle, Loving drove the remainder of the herd to the mining camps in Colorado. Despite the bad feeling that prevailed toward Texans, Goodnight and Loving had succeeded beyond their wildest dreams. As word of their success got back to Texas, countless other cattlemen followed, driving their beef-producing herds along the trail first blazed by Goodnight and Loving. Among them were John Chisum, John Dawson, and John Slaughter, whose names became immortalized in the lore of the Southwest. As the market competition increased in New Mexico, the Texas cattlemen sent their herds farther northward to meet the demands of the ranchers in Colorado and Wyoming. It is estimated that Goodnight delivered some thirty thousand head of cattle to this distant market over a three-year period.[8] For fourteen years, from 1866 to 1880, Texas cattlemen moved their longhorn herds westward and northward over the legendary Goodnight-Loving Trail. Ernest S. Osgood writes:

> To those who took part, accustomed as they became to all the possible incidents of the drive, near as they were with the solitudes over which they passed, each drive was a new adventure and its successful completion always brought to the most experienced something of the thrill of achievement. . . . To all those who saw that long line of Texas cattle come up over the rise in the prairies, nostrils wide for the smell of water, dust caked and gaunt, so ready to break from the nervous control of the riders strung out along the flanks of the herd,

7. Ibid.
8. Ibid., p. 259 (citing J. Evetts Haley, *Charles Goodnight,* p. 206).

there came the feeling that in this spectacle there was something elemental, something resistless, something perfectly in
keeping about the unconquered land about them.[9]

As the Texas cattlemen discovered the lush grama grass pastures
of New Mexico and the quality of the countryside for the production of cattle in large quantities, they moved in permanently with
their herds. Soon after, the Texans were followed by adventurous
folks from other states and even from foreign lands to try the cattle
business in the new El Dorado of the Southwest. The territory was a
public domain, except for what the United States treaty with Mexico
had guaranteed to its previous owners. The Pueblo Indians retained
some of the best valley lands, granted to them by the Spanish Crown
and confirmed to them by the Republic of Mexico following its independence from Spain. Some Hispanics held similar "grants." The rest,
tens of thousands of unfenced public acres, was free for the taking.
Longhorn cattle were tough and needed little care. Turned loose, they
grazed on the open range; if far from watering holes, they could go
several days without water and if grass was scarce, they could subsist
on desert plants.

Perhaps the best known and most intimidating early New Mexico
cattleman was John Chisum. Chisum, a Texan, established his headquarters near the Bosque Grande in 1873, controlling a range of some
150 miles along the Pecos from the Texas border to Fort Sumner,
where he held more water holes and hired more men than most. In
many respects, Chisum resembled a feudal monarch of the Middle
Ages and, according to one source, "his hired hands were as lawless
as any of the knights of old; if they did not carry broadswords and
lances, it was because their six-shooters were more effective."[10] He
became involved in the Lincoln County War, a conflict that pitted
large ranchers against small cattlemen and merchants and started
when a handful of cattlemen sneaked up the Pecos from Texas to con-
test Chisum's dominance. These cattlemen established the community of Seven Rivers and began to build their own herds, mostly from

---

9.   Osgood, *Day of the Cattleman*, p. 26.
10. Beck, p. 261 (citing William MacLeod Raine, *Cattles, Cowboys, and Rangers*, p. 160).

Hispanic cowboys near Las Cruces, NM, 1904.

Chuckwagon meal at Clayton, NM, c. 1915. (PHOTO BY CLAYTON STUDIO)

Chisum's strays. Chisum fought back, and, in the spring of 1877, the feud escalated into a shooting war.[11]

To the northeast in Colfax County, controversy over the legality of the Maxwell Land Grant erupted into a shooting war in the early 1870s when the new owners—an English-Dutch syndicate—attempted to run off the "squatters." With the agents of law enforcement on their side, the new owners had little difficulty winning eviction enforcement in court against those who were occupying farms, ranches, or mines. Carrying out the eviction notice, however, was an entirely different matter. It was only a matter of time before county residents polarized into two opposing factions—grant and anti-grant. While there were frequent feuds between the two sides, the real flare-up occurred in 1885, influenced by the shift in national politics. Fearing that the incoming Democratic administration of President Grover Cleveland might intervene on behalf of the settlers, the pro-grant faction appealed to the territorial governor early in 1885 for help to enforce the eviction decrees of the courts. With a nod from the governor, the land company organized a militia force composed of some thirty-five men under the leadership of James Masterson, a notorious gunman. The settlers, terrified of the band of hired killers, made a frantic appeal to the governor, who thereupon reversed his decision and ordered Masterson and his crew to disband and leave the territory.[12]

Toward the end of the century, cattlemen had grabbed up vast areas of New Mexico territory. Their great ranches dotted the eastern side, extending northward to the Colorado border, and some could also be found in the northwest corner and around Magdalena. Cattlemen dominated by the manipulation of water holes and, backed by well-armed riders, they doled out frontier justice to rustlers and trespassers alike. They faced a myriad of problems. First and foremost were the unremitting attacks by Apaches and Navajos, who were more often after horses than cattle. Next was the unrelenting thievery by the cattle rustlers. Much as the victim deplored it, cattle rustling was not a criminal offense and was often overlooked if the owners were the reviled Texans. On many occasions, the courts rendered decisions

11. Ibid., p. 260.
12. Ibid., pp. 170–171.

that made it virtually impossible for the foreigner (non–New Mexican) to have his stolen cattle returned to him. Sometimes, for that reason, Texan cattlemen took the law into their own hands and used force to deal out frontier justice to cattle thieves. The freewheeling days of the open range land in much of the territory ceased by the end of the nineteenth century. Mostly, it was the invention of barbed wire and the arrival of the railroads—trains from Iowa, Kansas, Missouri, and Arkansas—transporting into the territory homesteaders ("nesters," the ranchers called them) with legal claims, under the Homestead Act, to small plots. These factors combined to sound the death knell of the open range and the end of the unregulated use of government land by cattle barons.

MINING INDUSTRY

The story of gold mining in New Mexico was no more unusual than in most other western states. There was the same flurry of enthusiasm at the discovery of a new field, the wild stampede, and the influx of a large number of people seeking to hit it rich. Tent communities sprang up almost overnight in the remote regions where mineral deposits appeared. Many of them became towns, a few became cities, and others became ghost towns once the ore had been extracted.

The oldest mine in the United States was the Los Cerrillos, some twenty miles south of Santa Fe, where for generations Indians dug turquoise. The Spaniards paid little attention to the turquoise; Spain was mostly interested in gold and silver, and every explorer—doubting his predecessor's assurance that there was none—searched again. Many stories exist about mining in colonial times, but the supporting information is sketchy. According to one source, the first mining activity of lasting importance began about 1804, in the copper deposits of Santa Rita in the southwestern part of the state. For countless years the Indians had been digging copper from this mountain to fashion into crude utensils. In 1800, an Apache chief showed these copper deposits to his friend, Lieutenant Colonel José Manuel Carrasco, who filed a claim and named the place Santa Rita del Cobre. In 1804, Carrasco sold out to Don Manuel Elguea, a Chihuahua banker, who began to send burro trains of copper to Mexico for shipment to the royal mint in Spain. James Pattie leased this mine in 1822 and operated it successfully until he was bilked out of most of his working capital. Zebulon Pike, as well as other travelers, reported that the mine was in operation during the early nineteenth century. A Frenchman named Coursier worked the mine for seven years and reportedly cleared one million dollars from its operation; however, he was forced to abandon it as a result of Apache hostilities. It was not until the Indian menace was finally removed in the 1870s that it flourished again.[13] Gold was discovered in the Ortiz Mountains between Albuquerque and Santa Fe in 1828. Believed to be the oldest gold-mining district in the United States, gold valued at from sixty to eighty thousand dollars a year was extracted from this area between the years 1832 and 1835. By the time the Americans occupied New Mexico, the output was valued at about three million dollars. A group of Anglo-Americans took over mining at Ortiz in 1861 but were unable to operate it effectively because of the lack of water, a deficiency that continually plagued exploration of New Mexico's mineral resources.[14] The birth of gold mining in the territory occurred for the most part in the post–Civil War era. Colonel William Craig had heard stories of an old Spanish mine near Taos while he was stationed in the area before the war. Returning in 1869, he located the site of the mine, which was to open a field to the Arroyo Hondo.[15] Discoveries continued, and over the next few years gold was mined in twenty-three of the territory's thirty-two counties. The most important concentrations were in the Elizabethtown–Red River area that lay northeast of Taos on the western slope of Baldy Mountain in the Sangre de Cristo Range, and in the southwestern corner of the territory. But, compared to other western states, New Mexico never became an important center of gold production.

Magdalena and Socorro were the initial centers of silver mining beginning in 1863, but it was Silver City in the southwestern part of

13. Ibid., p. 244 (citing Margaret Meaders, "Copper Chronicle: The Story of New Mexico 'Red Gold,'" reprinted from *New Mexico Business*, vol. 12 [May and June 1958], p. 2).
14. Ibid., p. 245.
15. Ibid. (citing Pearson, "A New Mexican Gold Story," p. 175).

the state that became the primary producer. One of the richest finds was made in 1878, to the south of Hillsboro at Lake Valley, where, in the words of one writer, there was discovered "a vaulted cavern of horn silver so pure that miners sawed and cut the ore in blocks, instead of blasting it free."[16]

The crescendo of New Mexico's gold and silver mining boom had passed by the early 1890s, and, for a great many, dreams of finding the proverbial pot of gold at the end of the rainbow remained unrealized. As history has shown, one result of the search for gold and silver was that it attracted Anglo-Americans to the territory; once there and having failed to find their pot of gold, many lacked the means to return to their home states and settled down as farmers or ranchers, stimulating the territory's economic growth. Other mineral products have played a part in New Mexico's economic growth as well: coal and anthracite from near Cerrillos at Madrid and on the Maxwell Land Grant, natural gas in the Permian and the San Juan basins, and uranium in the area around Grants, and potash at Carlsbad. As New Mexico entered the twentieth century, the real giant of its mineral industry became petroleum. From modest beginnings in 1924, oil production steadily increased until, by mid-century, wells were pumping crude valued at nearly $300 million.

INDUSTRY AND TRANSPORTATION

Industry had little importance throughout much of New Mexico's history, mainly because of the area's remoteness and lack of transportation. From colonial times until the coming of the railroads, New Mexico was far removed from the centers of economic activity. With great distances between the settlements and the absence of navigable waterways, overland transportation, which was extremely slow and expensive, was the only means available.

The earliest means of transportation, and the one that lasted well into the nineteenth century, were pack animals, usually mules that

---

16. Simmons, *Interpretive History*, p. 159.

could carry loads up to four hundred pounds and were able to negotiate trails too steep for wagons or even horses.[17] The *carreta* became
more common during the Mexican era. It was a clumsy vehicle made
almost entirely from wood, there being little metal available. As one
writer described it:

> The wheels were solid blocks of wood sawed from the same
> tree, with a hole in the middle through which the axle was
> passed. . . . The axles were made of pine, and as there was no
> grease available, horrible sounds were emitted, and the mor-
> tality rate on axles was so high that at times it was necessary
> to half fill a cart with them. The bed and body of the cart was
> a rectangular block about four feet long and two and one-
> half feet wide. The wagon tongue was attached to the body
> with rawhide, and four posts were embodied in the corners
> of the body to hold the load. Oxen were attached by means
> of a yoke of timber placed directly on the heads of the oxen,
> behind the horns, and fastened with rawhide. Thus the cattle
> pushed, rather than pulled, heavy loads with their heads.[18]

These awkward carts were the mainstay of transportation until the
coming of the Anglo-Americans following General Kearny's occupation in the 1840s. Through necessity, Kearny upgraded the transportation system to accommodate the needs of the scattered frontier
garrisons throughout the territory. In the years following the Civil War,
John Butterfield's Overland Mail Route went far toward eliminating
the remoteness of New Mexico. Even after the arrival of the railroad
in 1879, stagecoaches were indispensable as feeder lines. Even into
the twentieth century, some of these stagecoach lines continued to
carry passengers, ceasing operations only when the automobile forced
them out of business.[19]

---

17. Beck, p. 275.
18. Ibid. (quoting James F. Meline, *Two Thousand Miles on Horseback*, p. 159; see also
    Max L. Morehead, "Spanish Transportation in the Southwest," *NMHR*, vol. 32
    [April 1957], p. 111).
19. Ibid., p. 279.

Carreta, c. 1846–47. (DRAWING BY LACHLAN ALLAN MACLEAN)

Stagecoach, "Mountain Pride" at Santa Fe, NM. (PHOTO BY LOM H. ROBERTS)

Traffic outside Palace of the Governors, Santa Fe in 1881. (ARTIST'S RENDITION)

AT and SF engine No. 137 at Gloria, NM, October 1880. (PHOTO BY BEN WITTICK)

Territorial Politics

For forty years after the Anglo-American occupation, the adobe royal city of Santa Fe was an army post, characterized by Erna Fergusson as "social, gossipy, and as brilliant as it could manage. . . . Bugle calls marked off the hours of day. . . . Sunday evenings, when the band played in the plaza, everybody went strolling there, or sat comfortably in victorias to watch others make the flirtatious circle."[20]

Although New Mexico had a predominantly Hispanic population, it was ruled by an elite group of Anglo-American political and business interests. The governor and other federal officials were party loyalists with claims on the president's patronage—not large claims, however, for remote New Mexico was not considered a choice political reward and appointees tended to be rather average. During territorial days, New Mexico was Republican because the national administration was usually in the hands of the Republicans. With the president responsible for appointing the governor and the other territorial officials, patronage was usually in Republican hands. Hispanic politics was a different matter, as the trappings of democracy, brought in by the Anglo-Americans, was not readily understood or even followed. The colonial system of *patrón*-peon continued. The patrón, used to dominating the life of the peon, did not automatically stop this practice after the Americans arrived. In each county, a few wealthy and influential Spanish families cooperated with the handful of Anglo-Americans to control the elections and handle government affairs. The illiterate peon voted for whom he was told to vote and found little time to bother himself with politics as long as his patrón looked after him.[21]

The railroads, completed in the late 1870s and early 1880s, made it much easier for more adventuresome would-be settlers to move to the territory and acquire land. As more newcomers arrived, the territory developed rapidly and land values increased accordingly. The mounting demand for homestead acreage brought into question the legitimacy of land grants made during the Spanish and Mexican

---

20. Fergusson, *Our Southwest,* p. 272.
21. Beck, p. 298 (citing Thomas C. Donnelly, *The Government of New Mexico,* p. 15).

periods to individuals or groups for meritorious public service. These grants were protected in the Treaty of Guadalupe Hidalgo (1848). However, in many instances the grants had become complicated by frequent transfers and subdivisions and, owing to general overall carelessness in the drawing up of the title papers, boundaries were unclear. All too frequently, lack of clarity in the title led to fraudulent documents, a circumstance made to order for the clever attorney.[22] The result was that many newcomers from the East, and even foreign investors, were defrauded by sellers lacking proper title to the land they sold.

Among the most celebrated cases was the Maxwell Grant of Colfax County, which ultimately embraced nearly two million acres and is believed to have been the largest tract of land ever held by a single owner in the United States. Charles Beaubien and Guadalupe Miranda jointly received the grant from Governor Armijo in the 1840s, apparently to encourage Mexican colonization of northern New Mexico. Lucien Maxwell came into possession of the property through marriage to Beaubien's daughter. He sold it in 1869 to an English syndicate, which, in turn, sold it in 1872 to a Dutch-English combine that went bust soon after. A lengthy and costly litigation arose over the rights of settlers who, throughout the 1870s and 1880s, continually harassed the owners by "squatting" on the land. Speculation in New Mexico land became a matter of national concern, prompting Congress to pass legislation setting up the Court of Private Land Claims in 1891. Its mandate was to settle land questions once and for all, and it succeeded in doing so by 1903. Appallingly, those who gained most from settlement of these land cases were often Anglo-American attorneys, many of whom collected their fees in land. Thomas B. Catron was one such land grant lawyer, acquiring more than two million acres of land and shared ownership in another four million acres. Catron, one of New Mexico's most powerful politicians, ended his career as one of the first two senators from New Mexico.[23]

---

22. Ibid., p. 174 (citing Bancroft, *Arizona and New Mexico*, p. 756, and the material on the land grant problem in the William Gillette Ritch Collection [Huntingham Library, San Marino, California]).

23. Roberts, p. 281.

Religion

Historians give greater attention to New Mexico's Catholic heritage than to the Protestant minority during the nineteenth century. This is because Catholicism was practically the only religion in the territory. It was not until the coming of the railroads, bringing Anglo-American settlers in large numbers, that the Protestant clergy were able to make an entry, usually following members of their own churches. The Baptists were the first in the area, arriving in Santa Fe in 1849; they built their first church there in 1854, the first Protestant church in New Mexico. Following the Baptists, the Presbyterians and the Methodists arrived in the 1850s. The earliest Episcopalian communities did not form until the late 1860s, and by the end of the century most of the other Protestant denominations had made their way into the territory. In some instances, the Protestants established mission stations and proselytized among the Indians on the reservations.

The first proselytizing effort by a Protestant group, according to Edward Spicer, occurred in the 1860s when the Church of Latter-day Saints (Mormons), through Jacob Hamblin, made a great effort to convert the Hopis. It was part of the Mormon belief that all American Indians were descendents of the Lamanites, one of the lost tribes of Israel. In accordance with this belief, they held that Indians had once practiced the Hebrew religion. It was therefore the duty of Mormons to convert Indians and bring them back on the right track. Although Hamblin worked on and off for six years among the Hopis and gained their friendship, he made no converts and gave up the task. The Mormon efforts made no more lasting impression on the Hopis than had the efforts of the Franciscans.[24] Jews began to arrive in New Mexico in the 1840s. They came as merchants and traders and at first their numbers were small; their first formal congregation was not organized until 1884. Two years later, Congregation Montefiore, an American Reform Congregation, built New Mexico's first synagogue at Las Vegas. Jews in Albuquerque formed Temple Albert in 1896. As these two towns grew, so did New Mexico's Jewish communities. The

---

24. Spicer, p. 517.

subject of religion in New Mexico would not be complete without mention of the Penitentes, properly called Los Hermanos de Luz (The Brothers of Light). A Roman Catholic religious society among Spanish Americans, its members are generally known for their practice of flagellation and the performance of a religious rite related mainly to the Lenten season. Each year during Holy Week, members would gather and reenact the Passion story. Erna Fergusson describes the self-torture associated with the passion ritual:

> Accompanied by the *pito* (flute), flagellants move in slow procession, their heads hidden in black sacks, their bare backs bleeding under the yucca lash and redly soaking their white cotton drawers. Bare feet are tortured on stones and thorns. No man cries out. One bears the heavy cross, falling as Jesus did, and often taking lashes from his fellows. Within memory, the *Cristo* was tied to the cross and left hanging there for minutes. Our grandfathers remembered seeing men nailed to the cross. There are reports of deaths and the tradition that a man's shoes, left on his doorstep, were the family's notice that he had died in holy penance.[25]

The origin of the Penitentes in New Mexico is unclear. According to some sources, they were an outgrowth of the Third Order of St. Francis, introduced by Franciscans sometime in the seventeenth century. Earlier rituals of flagellation, first introduced into Latin America during the sixteenth and seventeenth centuries, were far less severe than those adopted by New Mexicans in the early part of the nineteenth century.

The secret nature of Los Hermanos de Luz led to a great deal of misunderstanding of the organization's role and the extent of its influence. At times it exercised considerable political power among New Mexicans. It is believed to have played an influential role in the Taos uprising of 1847, and it was also influential, notwithstanding vigorous opposition, in the election of former priest Gallegos to several terms as New Mexico's territorial delegate to Congress. Condoned by

---

25. Fergusson, *Three Peoples*, p. 224.

the Church during much of its earlier history, Los Hermanos de Luz became most influential when priests were scarce, at which times officials of the group performed many of the functions of priests. Whenever the traditional ways of Spanish Americans were threatened with change, the Penitentes became, in the words of Erna Fergusson, "an organization of the common man against his masters—a brotherhood with temporal benefits and a pure solidarity and a secretiveness so relentless that it punishes betrayals of its laws and business with burial alive."[26] At the time when most of the clergy were driven out of New Mexico during the Mexican Revolution, the Penitentes moved in to fill the spiritual vacuum caused by the exodus of priests. In the aftermath of New Mexico's acquisition by the United States, and as their ritual practices grew increasingly more brutal, the Catholic Church became alarmed. This prompted Archbishop John B. Salpointe of Santa Fe (successor to Archbishop Lamy) to issue a circular letter in 1886 ordering them to abolish flagellation. When they ignored the order, a subsequent circular letter in 1889 ordered them to disband and prohibited their appearances in the churches. But the Penitentes persisted in their observances. Finally, in 1948, Archbishop Edwin V. Byrne imparted to them a blessing and the protection of the Church on the condition that they operate under Episcopal supervision.[27]

Los Hermanos de Luz still operate in Taos, Carmel, San Mateo and a few other places throughout New Mexico, although less openly and under the watchful eye of the archdiocese.

---

26. Beck, p. 220 (quoting Erna Fergusson, *Rio Grande,* p. 118).
27. Fergusson, *Three Peoples,* p. 214.

CHAPTER TWELVE

Lawlessness and Lawmen

The Lincoln County War of 1880 began with the killing of a wealthy émigré Englishman and concerned a cultivated Scotsman and a "boss" Irishman keeping store with a retired German officer.

—Erna Fergusson, *New Mexico: A Pageant of Three Peoples*

Throughout much of its territorial period, New Mexico wrestled with an epidemic of lawlessness, fueled by political infighting, range wars, land swindles, and cattle rustling unmatched in the history of America's western frontier. Outlaws stole horses and cattle and killed or got killed in the process. Farmers and ranchers engaged in frequent feuds, either against a neighbor's herd or a neighbor. When Governor Lionel A. Sheldon arrived in the territory, he found that desperados were virtually in control of the territory. He complained that "people were held up anywhere and everywhere, that stagecoaches were being robbed, and horses and cattle stolen." He was amazed to discover that, in many instances, the lawbreakers had the support of the people and even the cooperation of some law enforcement officials; bribing witnesses, and even judges, was so common it often went unnoticed.[1]

Much has been written, and many explanations given, about why New Mexico experienced so much lawlessness. Western historians often ascribe it to the unusual character of the New Mexican frontier that, unlike other frontiers, had an Anglo-American ethos superimposed an existing Hispanic way of life. This mixture, and the long-established hostility that existed between Hispanics and Anglos, is said

---

1. Beck, p. 160 (quoting from Hubert H. Bancroft Notes in Bancroft Library, University of California, Berkeley).

to have made the condition of general lawlessness more fragile and tenuous. This was particularly the case when the Anglos were Texans, for they had brought with them to New Mexico a well-developed sense of superiority and contempt toward Hispanics based on ethnic, cultural, and religious differences. Furthermore, mutual antagonism had its roots in history for, as Robert M. Utley describes it, "the Texas Revolution and the Mexican-American War had opened wounds not easily healed."[2] Other factors also contributed to New Mexico's lawlessness. First and foremost, there was the breed of characters that the frontier attracted—nonconforming, uncouth, and ruthless men eager to make their mark in the world. Nearly everyone carried firearms, and someone wronged, no matter how trivially, could lead to a shoot-out on the spot. There was inadequate enforcement of the laws, the blame for which is generally attributed to the federal government, which, in the words of one historian, "regarded the territory as an orphan among the nation's territories." The attitude in Washington was best summed up in General Sherman's remark: "We should have another war with old Mexico to make her take the territory back."[3] Military personnel and federal appointees resented being assigned to this most "undesirable" of all areas. For that reason, appointments to federal posts in the territory were the last ones filled, and they usually went to men who had been passed over for "juicier" political assignments.

GENERAL LAWLESSNESS

The era from the end of the Civil War to the end of the nineteenth century was one during which killings and lynchings were routine in New Mexico. Most communities had their legendary gunmen, such as Clay Allison, Elfego Baca, William "Billy the Kid" Bonney (Henry McCarty), Joe Fowler, and Thomas "Blackjack" Ketchum. Instead of being remembered as the cold-blooded killers they were, some of these gunslingers became folk heroes. Too frequently, lawlessness was

---

2.   Utley, *High Noon in Lincoln*, p. 21.
3.   Beck, p. 159.

not confined to six-shooter battles but found expression in common murder, even at times in political assassination. Every community had numerous gambling houses and the usual red light district. At one saloon in Cimarron, eleven patrons were reputed to have been killed in the course of a single month.[4]

Violent behavior seethed between Hispanics and Anglos. Elfego Baca despised the mistreatment of the Spanish Americans by incoming Texas cattlemen who were driving off Hispanic sheepherders. While Baca was campaigning to become sheriff of Frisco, a loathsome Texas cowboy named McCarthy went on a rampage, shooting up the town and intimidating the Hispanic natives. When the local justice of the peace declined to get involved out of fear, Baca confronted the Texan and arrested him. This did not sit well with the cowboy's fellow Texans, who gathered in mob force and demanded he release the prisoner. When Baca refused, an exchange of shots followed, killing one of the cowboys. The mob became enraged and attempted to arrest Baca for the murder of the cowboy. This led to a thirty-six-hour melee in which Baca is reputed to have single-handedly defended himself against eighty fuming Texans, killing four and wounding eight without receiving as much as a scratch himself. His feat has since been looked upon by Hispanics as one of the most heroic single-handed encounters in all six-shooter history.[5] The so-called Horrell War is another example. Five brothers named Horrell settled in Lincoln County in the spring of 1873 after they were chased out of Texas for committing a chain of cold-blooded murders. One night in December, as they engaged in the common pastime of shooting up Lincoln village and intimidating the Hispanic citizens, the constable tried to stop them. The ensuing gunfight resulted in the killing of the law officer and a Horrell gang member. In addition, one of the Horrells and another gang member were wounded and taken into custody, where their captors shot them in cold blood. In retaliation for this deed, the remaining Horrell brothers attacked a Hispanic wedding party on the night of December 10, murdering five of them. It is estimated that before the

---

4.   Ibid., p. 158.
5.   Ibid., p. 173.

gunfire was over, fourteen people were killed.[6] There were also many murders with political overtones. One notorious example was the slaying of Chief Justice John P. Slough of the territorial supreme court. Slough was shot down in La Fonda Hotel in Santa Fe in 1867 by William L. Rynerson[7] on the pretext that the judge had reached for his derringer first.[8] Also listed among the many crimes in New Mexico history were the deaths of Albert J. Fountain and his son. Fountain disappeared while en route from Lincoln to his home in Las Cruces in February 1896. Because he had been a judge, it was suspected that he met his death at the hands of political assassins. Indictments were returned, but no convictions were ever secured in the case.[9]

The Colfax County War (1875–1878) was another prominent disturbance that pitted claimants of the nearly two-million-acre Maxwell Land Grant against squatters, who had settled on what they regarded as public domain. At the center of the turmoil, which included a string of shootings and several hangings by enraged vigilantes, rode the notorious gunman Clay Allison. Allison had served as a scout for General Nathan Bedford Forrest during the Civil War, after which he migrated to Texas and became a cowhand for Oliver Loving and Charles Goodnight. By 1870, he was ranching in Colfax County and earning a reputation for getting into drunken brawls and gunfights. Legend has it that he once killed a man in a knife duel waged in an open grave that was to be occupied by the loser. On another occasion, he allegedly decapitated his victim and displayed the head in a Cimarron saloon. Allison met his end in a freak accident. He was thrown from a wagon and a rear wheel rolled over his head.[10]

Clayton, a favorite campground for cattle drovers on the northbound cattle trails, was the scene of a gruesome hanging in 1901. Thomas "Black Jack" Ketchum had migrated to Clayton from Texas, where he worked the surrounding ranches as a cowboy before he

6.   Ibid., p. 250.
7.   This was the same Rynerson who played a prominent role in the Lincoln County War.
8.   Beck, p. 173 (referencing Arie W. Poldervaart, *Black-Robed Justice,* p. 71).
9.   Ibid. (referencing Oliver LaFarge, *Santa Fe,* p. 159; George Curry, *Autobiography,* pp. 100–119).
10. Fugate and Fugate, pp. 236–237.

began specializing in train robberies. After the breakup of his gang, Black Jack tried to rob a train by himself but was wounded in the exchange of gunfire that ensued. He managed to escape but was captured the following day. Tried under the territorial laws of New Mexico, which carried the death penalty for train robbery, he was sentenced to hang. During his execution, which took place outside the Union County Courthouse on the afternoon of April 26, 1901, something went terribly wrong. When the trapdoor was sprung, Black Jack's head was wrenched from his body and it rolled toward the horrified spectators who had come to view the event. The quest for law and order in New Mexico was long and tedious. In many counties it was difficult to find men with sufficient courage to become sheriffs or deputies. Even the United States Cavalry had its hands full fighting the desperadoes.[11]

LINCOLN COUNTY WAR

The Lincoln County War was a struggle to determine whether an existing monopoly (the Murphy-Dolan-Riley party) or an aspiring monopoly (the Tunstall-Chisum-McSween faction) would dominate Lincoln County.[12] It was a conflict between newcomers and residents of long standing who had the officers of the law on their side. Favoritism for those well established constituted one of the primary problems of law enforcement.

The shooting death of an émigré Englishman on February 18, 1878, ignited the spark that touched off the Lincoln County War. John Henry Tunstall had arrived from England by way of Vancouver and San Francisco a year and a half earlier, hoping to make his fortune at cattle ranching. The Lincoln into which Tunstall arrived was already a violent world, festering with hostility that regularly upset the peace of the county. The county seat, Lincoln (formally La Placita), was an adobe village of four hundred people, mostly Hispanic, that extended about a mile on both sides of a single street; at its western edge stood

11. Ibid., p. 171.
12. Ibid., p. 112.

Lawrence G. Murphy's "big store," the only two-story building in town. Nine miles upstream from Lincoln at Fort Stanton, the army stood watch over the Mescalero Apache Indians, whose reservation and agency lay across the divide to the southwest. Together, the agency and the fort provided virtually the only market for the farmers and stockmen in the county. Major Lawrence G. Murphy, one of the men chiefly responsible for the war, was an Irish immigrant in his middle forties and veteran of two enlistments in the regular army and commissioned service with the New Mexico volunteers. He had come to Fort Stanton at the close of the Civil War and, in partnership with another Civil War officer, a German named Emil Fritz, had set himself up as trader at the fort. Here and at a small branch store in Lincoln, the partners served both military and civilian customers.[13] A cunning businessman, Murphy rapidly built a lucrative business enhanced by profitable contracts supplying meat and merchandise to Fort Stanton. As his commercial activity and financial means grew, his economic and political grasp on the community also grew; farmers and ranchers were forced to do business with him at inflated prices. Men who stood up to Murphy, one citizen remarked, "were either killed or run out of the County." The sheriff was his man, as were the local district attorney, William Rynerson, and the United States district attorney at Santa Fe, Thomas B. Catron. It was alleged that even the territorial governor, Samuel Axtell, was beholden to him. By such means, Lawrence Murphy was able to dominate the economic life and control the law in the surrounding countryside.[14] But there were also people who were highly antagonistic toward him. Most prominent among them were the Englishman John Tunstall, Texas cattleman John Chisum, owner of one of the largest ranches in New Mexico, and lawyer Alexander McSween, a Canadian-born Scotsman. Many other people in the community were likewise dissatisfied with Murphy. Indicative of this was the large number of grand jury indictments growing out of the Lincoln County War that were returned against Murphy and his supporters.[15] Alexander McSween arrived in Lincoln in 1875, by way

---

13. Utley, *High Noon in Lincoln*, p. 14.
14. Keleher, *Violence in Lincoln County: 1869–1881*, p. 149.
15. Beck, p. 165.

*Lincoln County Courthouse, c. 1905, previously the Murphy-Dolan store.
It was from here that Billy the Kid made his spectacular escape on
April 28, 1881.*

of Kansas. Although he was a lawyer, he had been trained for the Presbyterian ministry and, unlike most of Lincoln's citizens, did not touch alcohol or wear a gun. Murphy's opponents found McSween to be a man capable of leading them and he was soon busy handling legal cases against Murphy, many of them on behalf of cattleman Chisum. But McSween was ambitious and in due course was engaging in activities beyond the practice of law. With financial backing, purportedly from Chisum and Tunsdall, he acquired an interest in a ranch, started the county's first official bank and then built a store to challenge the trade monopoly Murphy had long enjoyed.[16] These moves earned him the enmity of Murphy and confrontation was inevitable. Certain others figured prominently in the events of the Lincoln County War: Jimmy Dolan and John Riley were two of Murphy's fellow Irishmen who became partners in the business when ill health forced Murphy to move to Santa Fe for medical treatment. They were supported by a gang of outlaws, a band of some thirty or forty horse and cattle thieves headed by Lincoln County's most accomplished cutthroat, Jesse Evans. Evans, a Texan, had served as one of Chisum's horse thieves for several years before becoming one of the more notorious Murphy-Dolan-Riley gunmen. He broke out of the Fort Stanton lockup in March 1879 and returned to Texas where he was subsequently sentenced to ten years in the penitentiary for killing a Texas Ranger. While serving time, however, he walked away from a work gang and vanished into the unknown.[17]

The Lincoln County conflict arose over a legal matter—insurance money owed from the estate of Emil Fritz, Murphy's former partner, who had died after returning to Germany. This policy, totaling $10,000, was turned over to McSween for collection with the understanding that his fee would not exceed $2,500. According to historians, McSween encountered such difficult legal questions in the collection of the policy that the insurance company was reluctant to make payment. McSween was obliged to go to New York, where he later claimed he was forced to pay $2,500 to lawyers and $4,095 for out-of-pocket expenses. Suspecting that McSween had fleeced them, Fritz's heirs took the matter to Murphy, who recommended that they

---

16. Ibid.
17. Utley, *High Noon in Lincoln*, p. 167.

ask U.S. Attorney Thomas B. Catron and District Attorney William L. Rynerson to look into the matter. Legal action followed, and McSween was charged with embezzlement. His property, worth $100,000, was attached for the amount of the $8,000 due, and bond was set at $16,000. Furthermore, John Tunstall's property, valued at $50,000, was attached on the grounds that McSween had an interest in his business dealings. It was during the process of seizing Tunstall's property that the first volley in the Lincoln County War was fired. Tunstall, overtaken by a sheriff's pose, was fired upon and killed. According to the official version, he died while resisting arrest; according to other versions, he was shot down in cold blood. It was later alleged by the McSween faction that the Murphy-Riley-Dolan group had planned his murder and also intended to murder McSween to eliminate them as business rivals. Circulars were distributed in Lincoln County accusing a group including William Brady, Thomas B. Catron, and William L. Rynerson, in addition to Riley and Dolan, with having been in on the "plot." To corroborate the claims, a letter (suspected to be a forgery) from Rynerson to Riley and Dolan turned up, stating: "It must be made too hot for Tunstall and his friends, the hotter the better, shake that McSween outfit up till it shells out and squares up and then shake it out of Lincoln."[18]

Knowing that justice was not to be had from Lincoln County sheriff Brady, the McSween faction turned to Justice of the Peace Wilson, who issued warrants for the arrest of the men identified as the murderers. For daring to side with the McSween group, Governor Samuel Axtell (a friend of Murphy) removed Wilson from his office on a trumped-up charge. Later testimony showed that those who wanted to act impartially had been warned from Santa Fe that their own activities would be open to scrutiny if they dared offer assistance to any but the Murphy group. Despairing of ever getting the law to back them, the McSween-Chisum faction decided to take matters into their own hands. In early March 1878, members of the faction killed two members of the posse that had allegedly murdered Tunstall. They struck again several weeks later, shooting down Sheriff William Brady and his deputy, George Hindman. Sheriff Brady had

18. Keleher, p. 81.

ties to the "House" (as the Murphy establishment was called); he and Murphy had been friends for years, since serving together in the war. Although he did not take orders from Murphy, he could usually be counted on to do what Murphy wanted. Brady, a respected citizen, "made the fourth of a band of fraternal Irishmen, three of them ex-soldiers, all hard drinkers, and none, given their sense of the anti-colonial struggle in Ireland, with any great affection for Protestant Englishmen or Scotsmen."[19] Brady and his deputy were gunned down the morning of April 1, 1878. Among the killers (members of the McSween-Chisum faction) was Henry McCarty,[20] alias William Bonney. People called him Kid, and one day he would be known as the legendary Billy the Kid. Billy had witnessed the murder of his friend Tunstall and vowed to take revenge. Believing that Brady and Hindman were implicated in his death, Billy and several companions gunned the lawmen down one early morning as they were on their way to the Lincoln courthouse. McSween and his group succeeded in having their man, John S. Copeland, named to succeed Brady. However, Governor Axtell found an excuse to block the appointment and selected George Peppin, a Murphy-Dolan-Riley man, instead. There were more clashes and killings, prompting Governor Axtell to make an appeal to President Hayes for federal troops. On June 29, the post commander at Fort Stanton announced his troops could not participate in quelling civil disturbances because Congress had forbidden such action. With intervention by the army ruled out, McSween decided it was time to seize the initiative. On July 14, he assembled some sixty followers in and around his Lincoln residence, and what would become known as the "Five-Day Battle" began.

The next day, Sheriff Peppin moved about forty men into the Wortley Hotel down the street from the McSween house. For the next two days there was sporadic fighting, during which gunfire and verbal insults were exchanged. On the fourth day, the commander of

---

19. Ibid., p. 30 (quoting from Widenmann biographical notes, Mullin Collection, Haley Library and History Center, Midland, TX).

20. Henry was one of two sons born to Catherine McCarty, who had arrived in New York from Ireland during the potato famine period. She later moved west, first to Indiana, where she met Henry Antrim, and later to New Mexico, where they were married.

William H. Bonney, aka Billy the Kid, c. 1879.

Fort Stanton arrived with a force of thirty-five men and five officers equipped with a mountain howitzer and a Gatling gun.[21] Although the troops did not intervene, their presence was enough to intimidate the McSween forces, some of whom quietly dispersed. On July 19, day five of the siege, the sheriff torched the McSween house, and, as the flames spread throughout the interior, the occupants were forced to evacuate. During the mass evacuation, McSween and several of his supporters were killed. The rest managed to escape, including Billy the Kid, who took command of coordinating an escape plan when it became clear that lives were at risk.

WAR'S END

After the Five-Day Battle, President Hayes bowed to political pressure from influential individuals within the territory and replaced Governor Axtell with the celebrated Lew Wallace, who became better known as the author of the novel *Ben Hur*. Arriving in Santa Fe in September 1878, Wallace issued a proclamation that was published in the *Santa Fe Sentinel* on November 14, 1878, pronouncing "amnesty for all of those who would give testimony and desist from further disorders," precipitately announcing "that the disorders lately prevalent in Lincoln County . . . have been happily brought to an end." The amnesty aroused a flood of public criticism, and on March 6, 1879, Wallace went to Lincoln, where he spent time interviewing the various participants.

Before his arrival, however, the tragedy of the Lincoln County War had claimed yet another victim. This time it was a lawyer by the name of Houston Chapman, who had come to Lincoln to close out the McSween estate. At the same time, the new sheriff, George Kimball, had convened the leaders of the warring factions to seek ways to end the feuding and restore harmony in the county. After getting everyone to agree to shake hands and make up, Kimball then made the mistake of inviting them all to a nearby saloon for a few drinks. Leaving the saloon, Chapman purportedly made a disparaging remark

---

21. Fugate and Fugate, p. 307.

to Jimmy Dolan, for which he was gunned down by Jesse Evans, one of the more notorious Murphy-Riley-Dolan gunmen.[22]

PURSUIT AND CAPTURE OF BILLY THE KID

Lincoln County acquired Pat Garrett as its sheriff in the election of 1880. Garrett at once set out to capture Billy the Kid and, shortly before Christmas 1880, managed to corner him and his gang at Stinking Springs near Fort Sumner. The Kid surrendered and was lodged in a jail cell in Santa Fe to await trial. He was tried in Mesilla in April 1881, where the jury quickly convicted him of the murders of Brady and Hindman, and the judge ordered him returned to Lincoln and hanged.

While awaiting his execution, Billy escaped from the Lincoln County courthouse, killing his guards, Charles Robert Olinger and J. W. Bell, in the process. (Olinger was a bully, whose lust for blood was evident from his many gruesome deeds. When the Lincoln County War erupted, the Murphy-Dolan-Riley group hired him. He was among the posse that had ambushed and killed the unarmed John Tunstall in a lonely ravine near Pajarito Spring.) The Kid detested Olinger, who took perverse pleasure in tormenting his prisoner. At noon on April 28, 1881, while Olinger was escorting other prisoners to a nearby eating place for lunch, the Kid asked Bell to take him to the lavatory behind the courthouse. There, he picked up the pistol that a friend had left for him and, on his way back to his cell, shot and killed Bell. He then scooped up a double-barreled shotgun which Olinger had left lying on a nearby table and, as the bully sprinted across the street toward the courthouse, the Kid gave him both barrels, killing him instantly.[23] For three months, Garrett and his deputies doggedly pursued the Kid, the trail leading eventually to the Kid's favorite haunts around Fort Sumner and finally to the darkened bedroom of Billy's friend, Pete Maxwell. There on the night of July 14, 1881, Garrett pumped two bullets into the chest of his quarry and the

22. Beck, p. 169 (citing Ralph E. Twitchell, *Leading Facts,* vol. 2, p. 425).
23. Ibid., p. 164.

Kid fell, mortally wounded. The Lincoln County War ended with fifty or more indictments. Not all who were indicted stood trial, and only one was convicted of a crime—Billy the Kid, for the murder of Sheriff Brady. In the view of some, Wallace did, however, help bring about a final resolution to the conflict through capable leadership. By aggressively pursuing the outlaws and using the military and his own militia, he helped to breathe new life into the institutions of government and rekindle the confidence of the people in those institutions.[24]

---

24. Utley, *High Noon in Lincoln*, p. 158.

CHAPTER THIRTEEN

Reaching for the Forty-seventh Star

New Mexico entered the 20th century seeking statehood and self-government after more than 50 years as a territory run by appointed governors. It was a conquered land.

—Larry Calloway, *Albuquerque Journal*

New Mexico's long struggle for statehood was finally achieved on January 6, 1912. It was a jubilant occasion for the New Mexican delegation present in Washington when President William H. Taft signed the proclamation formally admitting New Mexico to the Union as the forty-seventh state. After signing the historic document, the president turned to the delegation and said, "Well, it is all over. I am glad to give you life. I hope you will be healthy."[1] When the news of statehood was flashed in Santa Fe, "a large crowd assembled and cheered itself hoarse over the victory for which New Mexico had been fighting for three score years."[2]

No other state had fought so vigorously to be admitted to the Union or, for that matter, had as many setbacks. There was barely a congressional session between 1849 and 1910 without a bill for statehood; in all, some fifty bills were introduced during the sixty-year struggle.[3] Many reasons have been given as to why it took New

---

1. Simmons, *Interpretive History,* p. 167 (quoting Robert W. Larson, *New Mexico's Quest for Statehood, 1846–1912,* p. 304).

2. Beck, p. 241 (quoting *Santa Fe New Mexican,* June 20, 1910, in Oliver La Farge, *Santa Fe,* p. 199).

3. In sorting out New Mexico's enduring struggle to achieve statehood, I have relied heavily on the works of historians Bancroft and Beck.

Mexico so long to become a state. Some suggest that early efforts were hampered by general ignorance about the territory and suspicions toward its people. Others believe that statehood was opposed by those who felt that New Mexico's predominantly Hispanic and Indian populations were "too foreign" and "too Catholic" for admission to the American Union. There were also questions about the loyalty these recently conquered people had for their new country. The loyalty issue was eventually laid to rest by the commendable service of New Mexicans in support of the Union cause during the Civil War and later in the Spanish-American War.[4] After the Civil War the many bills for New Mexico's statehood were blocked, among other reasons, because of the bitter antagonism over Reconstruction and the East's fear of Western domination in the Senate. Historian Beck believes that the blame did not rest solely with Washington. He writes:

> Much of the responsibility for the monotonous succession of failures must be attributed to conditions within New Mexico itself. From the very inception of the battle for statehood, many were opposed to it, preferring territorial status instead. Usually, the mining interests, the large merchants, the railroads and some of the bigger landowners were opposed to statehood because it would mean higher taxes. And as territorial politics were usually influenced by these groups, they provided potent opposition.[5]

Path to Statehood

Shortly after the United States acquired the territory in 1848, New Mexico made its first unsuccessful bid for statehood. In the fall of 1849, nineteen delegates attended a "convention" in Santa Fe where they drafted a plan for territorial government and elected one of their members, Hugh N. Smith, as the territory's delegate to Congress. This

---

4. Robert J. Torrez, "A Cuarto Centennial History of New Mexico," New Mexico State Records Center and Archives, Sante Fe, New Mexico.
5. Beck, p. 226.

effort failed when the House refused to seat Smith as the territorial delegate.[6]

On March 4, 1849, Major General Zachary Taylor, a popular military hero, became president. Without delay, he made known his administration's desire to bring both New Mexico and California into the Union in an attempt to head off the slavery controversy and, in the case of New Mexico, to help resolve the thorny problem of the Texas claim to the Rio Grande.[7] With expectations high and the Taylor administration on its side, New Mexico called a constitutional convention in the spring of 1850. This convention drafted a constitution copied largely from those adopted by some of the newer middle-western states. Without waiting for approval from Washington, New Mexicans took it upon themselves to hold elections immediately and implement the state government. Conceivably, they were deluded into thinking that approval was a foregone conclusion, and, according to some historians, it may well have been had it not been for the untimely death of President Taylor on July 9, 1850. The succession of Millard Fillmore to the presidency and the new course of national politics constituted a setback for the infant state government. Additionally, the process by which the election was conducted and the notoriety surrounding it persuaded many that the territory was not ready for statehood.[8] In the meantime, a California petition for admittance to the Union was blocked by Southern states because its constitution included a clause prohibiting slavery. A compromise, known as the Compromise of 1850, consisting of five bills, emerged. These bills admitted California to the Union as a free state, organized New Mexico and Utah without any restriction on slavery, set the boundaries of Texas, reimbursing Texas ten million dollars for relinquishing

---

6. Beck, p. 228 (citing Twitchell, *Leading Facts,* vol. 2, pp. 269–270; Twitchell attributes this setback to the intrigues of the Southerners).

7. For additional treatment of this dispute, see "Boundary Disputes and Adjustments" in Chapter 8, "The United States Takes Control."

8. While 90 percent of the delegates to the 1850 constitutional convention was composed of Spanish Americans, those selected to run and represent the state (the two senators, the governor, and the lieutenant governor) were all Anglos, with the exception of Manuel Alvarez, who was from Spain. Beck, p.229 (citing Ralph E. Twitchell, *Leading Facts,* vol. 2, p. 277).

claims to land belonging to New Mexico, abolished slave trade in the District of Columbia, and provided a new Fugitive Slave Act, strengthening the act of 1793 with federal jurisdiction. Although Taylor had threatened to veto the compromise measures, his death deferred final decision to his successor, President Fillmore. Fillmore, unlike his predecessor, favored the compromise measures and signed them into law. The outcome of the compromise was that California was admitted to the Union as the thirty-first state. The balance of the Mexican secession of 1848 was divided at the thirty-seventh parallel into the territories of Mexico and Utah. The Texas–New Mexico boundary dispute was settled, with Texas relinquishing its claims to part of the New Mexico Territory. President Fillmore appointed Indian agent James S. Calhoun as the first territorial governor on March 3, 1851, leaving the forces for statehood to resign themselves to a territorial form of government for the time.

Circumstances of the Elkins Handshake

In spite of several subsequent attempts, it was 1875 before the next serious move was made to push the statehood issue onto the congressional agenda. This time it would be lost as a result of the legendary "Elkins Handshake." Stephen B. Elkins, New Mexico's Republican territorial delegate to Congress, succeeded in gaining sufficient votes to have the statehood measure passed in both the House and the Senate. As the bill made its way back to the House for action on some minor Senate amendments, it appeared that statehood was all but achieved. At the very same time, however, the House was engaged in an acrimonious debate over reconstruction measures for the South. During debate on one of the bills, Congressman Julius Caesar Burroughs of Michigan made a highly upsetting speech, extremely critical of the South and rehashing its "crimes of secession." Delegate Elkins, who was not present for the speech, entered the House chamber as a group of Northern congressmen gathered around Burroughs to congratulate him. Unaware of the contents of the speech, Elkins shook Burroughs's hand and also complimented him. Southern members, observing the handshake, were infuriated, as it appeared to them that Elkins was in fact endorsing Burroughs's position. They decided to get even by withdrawing their support for the final version of the New Mexico statehood measure.[9] Once again New Mexico had failed in its bid for statehood, only this time it failed because of a handshake. Notwithstanding Colorado's admission to the Union the following year, New Mexico would remain a territory for another thirty-six years. In the intervening period, New Mexicans were as determined as ever to push ahead in their quest for statehood. The next serious statehood measure taken under consideration by Congress came in 1888. It was known as the Omnibus Bill, and it provided for the admission of not only New Mexico but also the territories of Dakota, Montana, and Washington. North and South Dakota, Montana, and Washington were promptly admitted; Idaho and Wyoming were admitted the following year. New Mexico failed yet another time, despite the fact that her population was larger than that of most of those states. But, as one observer noted, the citizens of the other states for the most part spoke English and were predominantly Protestant.

ROLE OF THE NATIONAL PRESS

The drama of New Mexico's failed statehood attempts attracted the attention of the national newspapers; much of what was written, moreover, opposed statehood for a variety of narrow-minded reasons. Some of it was because of antagonism toward the Catholic Church and resentment toward the Spanish-speaking inhabitants "who have not troubled to learn English."[10] One journal asserted that the "Romish priesthood" would so completely dominate the state as to make successful government impossible.[11] Much was made of the bilingualism of the people, as well as the general lawlessness that existed. The *Chicago Tribune*

9.　Beck, p. 230 (citing Ralph E. Twitchell, *Leading Facts,* vol. 2, pp. 404–406).

10.　Ibid., p. 231 (quoting from the *Rocky Mountain News* [Denver], February 18, 1875, in Ritch Scrapbook).

11.　Ibid. (quoting the *New York Observer,* March 9, 1876, in Ritch Scrapbook).

observed that "New Mexico has but a few oases amid its volcanic deserts." The *Milwaukee Sentinel* of April 6, 1876, wrote:

> If any geographical division of this country were to be selected for the final jumping off place for the American citizen, it would surely be New Mexico. A man could pass into the mysteries and doubts of his future existence in that region with perfect equanimity. The change could hardly be for the worse. It comprises the tag end of all that is objectionable in an imperfect civilization. The scum and dregs of the American, Spanish, Mexican and Indian people are there concentrated. . . . In making this assertion we do not mean to include those exceptions that prove the rule. There are doubtless a limited number of respectable people in New Mexico, but the number is so small comparatively that it could no more control the politics of the proposed state than a rowboat could sink the *Great Eastern*. The mass of the inhabitants— half-breeds, "greasers," "outlaws," etc—are no more fit to support a proper state government than they are to run the missions.[12]

QUEST CONTINUES

Despite innumerable racial, religious, political, and economic issues that delayed every attempt at statehood, New Mexico's quest for admission to the Union continued. A state constitutional convention, convened in the fall of 1889, drafted a new constitution. However, the voters were not satisfied with the new document and rejected it in October of the following year. The reasons for rejection apparently had nothing to do with the merits of statehood. The Democrats strongly opposed it because, in their opinion, they were not given adequate representation at the convention. The Catholic Church opposed it because it provided for the establishment of nonsectarian public schools.

---

12. Ibid. (quoting from the *Milwaukee Sentinel*, April 6, 1876, in Ritch Scrapbook).

Finally, according to Marion Dargan, the Anglo constituents rejected it because they feared being overwhelmed by the native "Mexicans."[13]

Undaunted, New Mexicans doggedly pursued their goal. In the period between December 1891 and June 1903, some twenty statehood bills were introduced in Congress. A few made it through the House; none got through the Senate. Hope was rekindled in 1899, when Teddy Roosevelt arrived in Las Vegas, New Mexico, for a boisterous first reunion with his "Rough Riders,"[14] most of whom had come from New Mexico. On that occasion, Roosevelt declared, "All I shall say is if New Mexico wants to be a state, you can count me in, and I will go back to Washington to speak for you or do anything you wish."[15]

Theodore Roosevelt had an opportunity to back his words with action when, in September 1901, he became president after an assassin's bullet cut down President McKinley. But Roosevelt, the man who had led the Rough Riders on a daring charge in the battle of San Juan Hill, failed to keep the promise he had made at Las Vegas. As one authority put it, "Roosevelt the Rough Rider and Roosevelt the politician were not always in agreement." Naturally, New Mexicans were disappointed, but it did not discourage them from making another try. A bill was submitted in May 1902 to admit Arizona, New Mexico, and Oklahoma. It passed the House but ran into strong opposition in the Senate by Senator Albert J. Beveridge, chairman of the Committee on Territories. Political rivals described Beveridge as a man "obsessed with a desire to keep New Mexico out of the Union and (he) made a veritable crusade of it."[16] The reason for Beveridge's opposition to New Mexico entering the Union is not altogether clear. Warren A. Beck maintains he was not a religious bigot, nor was he opposed to statehood on racial grounds. He was known to have made occasional reference to the fact that the people of New Mexico were of different racial and linguistic backgrounds from the rest of the country, but, as

---

13. Ibid., p. 232 (citing Marion Dargan, "New Mexico's Fight for Statehood," *NMHR*, vol. 18 [January 1943], p. 66).

14. The name given to the 1st U.S. Volunteer Cavalry, which Roosevelt led in the Spanish-American War.

15. Quoted in Fugate and Fugate, p. 152.

16. Beck, p. 234.

Beck and others point out, he approved territorial status for the Philippines, where there were more than ten million people who could not speak English.[17] What then was the basis for Beveridge's opposition to New Mexico statehood? One authority wrote, "Beveridge was motivated primarily by the conviction that the creation of a state concerns the nation and not alone the territory involved."[18] He believed that it was not fair to the nation as a whole to give the small western areas the status of statehood before they were prepared for it. His consistency in this view has not been addressed. Beveridge continued to play for time as the backers of New Mexico statehood gained momentum. As chairman of the Committee on Territories, he was able to block efforts to bring the matter to a vote.

Attempt to Join New Mexico and Arizona

As pressure for New Mexico statehood continued to mount, Beveridge (recognizing that he could not hold out indefinitely) considered the idea of jointure. In 1905, he endorsed legislation calling for Oklahoma and the Indian Territory to be admitted as one state and for New Mexico and Arizona to be admitted as another. The bill combining New Mexico and Arizona into a single state passed Congress and was signed by President Theodore Roosevelt in 1906. Jointure was accepted by Oklahoma Territory and the Indian Territory, and it was assumed that New Mexico and Arizona would follow suit. This, without question, would have happened, except for an amendment by Senator Joseph B. Foraker of Ohio stipulating that joint admission would take effect only if it were ratified by a majority of the voters in each territory.[19]

Most New Mexicans prepared to accept this measure as necessary in order to get into the Union. Only a few New Mexicans, led by Governor Miguel A. Otero, opposed joint statehood. New Mexico

17. Ibid. (citing Edwin R. Bingham, *Charles F. Lummis: Editor of the Southwest*).
18. Ibid. (citing Claude G. Bowers, *Beveridge and the Progressive Era,* p. 196).
19. The reason Senator Foraker submitted his amendment was his concern that the larger population in New Mexico would dominate. See Beck, p. 238.

accepted the measure by an overwhelming margin. However, Arizona preferred to wait for single statehood rather than join the dominant Spanish-speaking element of New Mexico and voted overwhelmingly against the measure. In the aftermath, President Roosevelt wrote Senator Beveridge: "I do feel very strongly that no good whatever comes with any further delay. You will have to take them both in. You cannot take them both in together and by keeping them out for a short time, which is all you can do, you merely irritate the people there against the Republican party."[20] Roosevelt's successor, President William Taft, was confronted head-on with the issue while visiting New Mexico in 1909, during the first year of his administration. At a reception in his honor in Albuquerque, he was reminded in a speech by Albert B. Fall, one of the territory's ablest political leaders, of the long history of past broken promises of statehood. To the dismay of the gathering, Fall sarcastically remarked that Taft, their distinguished guest, was no exception. Though not scheduled to speak, the president got up and expressed regret for Washington's past lack of action on statehood, concluding his remarks: "Judge Fall, I have heard your argument and am for your cause in spite of it."[21]

FINAL STRETCH

The president's commitment and the resulting publicity undeniably aided the cause for statehood, for in January 1910 the House passed the Hamilton Bill, the enabling act for statehood in New Mexico (and Arizona). In the Senate, it was referred to the Committee on Territories, where Senator Beveridge, New Mexico's old nemesis, had a change of heart. Resigned to the inevitable, he and his committee undertook to write a statehood bill that "would be in the public interest." When some eastern senators opposed some of the protective features that Beveridge had written into the bill, the senator found

---

20.　Beck, p. 239 (citing Claude G. Bowers, *Beveridge and the Progressive Era,* p. 268).

21.　Ibid. (quoting George Curry, *Autobiography,* pp. 245–246; David H. Stratton, "Albert B. Fall and the Teapot Dome Affair" [Ph.D. dissertation, University of Colorado, 1955], pp. 35–37).

himself fighting for New Mexican statehood with the same tenacity with which he had previously opposed it. The enabling act passed both houses of Congress and was signed into law by President Taft on June 20, 1910. After a constitutional convention comprising delegates from every county in the territory, an acceptable constitution was drafted and Congress passed the statehood measure. On January 6, 1912, President Taft formally announced the admission of New Mexico as the forty-seventh state of the Union, and the citizens of the new state rejoiced. A few days later on January 15, 1912, William C. McDonald stood on the steps of the capitol building in Santa Fe and was inaugurated as the first governor of the State of New Mexico.

New Mexico State Constitutional Convention, Territorial Capitol, Santa Fe, NM, 1910. (PHOTO BY WILLIAM R. WALTON)

William McDonald, New Mexico's first state governor, in his office in the state capitol, 1912.

CHAPTER FOURTEEN

Beyond Statehood

To understand properly the politics of New Mexico it is necessary to remember that the state "may be in the United States but is not of the United States," for the political history of New Mexico is unlike that of any other of the fifty states.

—Warren A. Beck, *New Mexico: A History of Four Centuries*

It was the arrival of the railroads in the late nineteenth century more than any other event that ended the centuries of isolation that had beset New Mexico since the Europeans first reached there and revealed the area to the outside world. The railroads made it easier for the more adventuresome would-be settlers to move to the territory and acquire land. Countless feeder lines to the more remote areas made possible the settlement of many parts of the state that would otherwise have remained empty. As more newcomers arrived, the population expanded and the economy slowly improved.

Not all newcomers arrived by rail. Typical was Walter Moncus who, in the summer of 1902, loaded his wife, infant son, and their belongings into two covered wagons and headed northwest from Texas, planning to settle in Arizona. He hoped to homestead somewhere near present-day Phoenix. A chance meeting along the way persuaded him to change his mind and opt instead for New Mexico. At a place called Chaco Canyon, Walter and his wife found a live spring and staked a claim. They were the only Anglo homesteaders in the area, but others would soon follow.

The New Mexico into which Walter arrived, despite the American takeover in 1848, was still heavily Spanish speaking. In the early twentieth century, more than 87 percent of the Spanish-speaking population of the Southwest still lived in the valleys along the Rio Grande, where their ancestors had first appeared in 1598. Their culture was older than that of Walter and Isabel Moncus; older still than the Anglo culture of New England or Virginia.[1] New Mexico was chiefly a rural state until the 1940s. In 1890, the state's population was 94 percent rural, declining to 82 percent by 1920. By 1940, partly due to the Depression, the majority of those living on the land had further declined to 67 percent. This trend continued after World War II, as folks from the rural areas headed for Albuquerque and other growing urban areas to seek work in postwar military installations and industries relating to atomic research and special weapons programs.

Early Statehood Years

New Mexico's successful conclusion to a long and hard-fought campaign to achieve full participation in the Union did not instantly solve all of the territory's problems. To quote Marc Simmons: "All together . . . but not quite."[2] Sporadic periods of violence began to develop among the Pueblo Indians, Spanish speakers, and Anglos over land rights. The source of the unrest stemmed from the Treaty of Guadalupe Hidalgo, which guaranteed the Pueblo Indians all land rights granted them by the Spaniards. The Pueblos were constantly beset by non-Indians acquiring parcels of their lands, regardless of the treaty provision. This was due in some measure to an 1876 U.S. Supreme Court decision that ruled that the Pueblo Indians, owing to their highly developed culture, were not dependants of the federal government and, further, held title to their lands, which they could dispose of at will.

Deprived of government financial assistance and without the federal protection from which they had previously derived benefit, individual members began selling off small parcels of their Indian land and, in a matter of time, some 30 percent or more of the Pueblos' best acreage had passed into non-Indian hands. No doubt the Pueblos'

---

1. Nugent, *Into the West,* p. 200.
2. Simmons, *Interpretive History,* p. 168.

land base would have continued to erode had not the Supreme Court, in a 1913 decision, reversed its earlier stand and ruled that the United States government was, in fact, responsible for the guardianship of the Pueblo peoples. Moreover, the Court ruled that such responsibility was continuous since the acquisition of the territory by the United States. Furthermore, all losses of original Pueblo lands to encroachers or purchasers were illegal.[3] Sadly, many non-Indian trespassers disregarded the Court's decision, contending that their families had acquired the land in good faith. In fact, some Hispaños and Anglos had lived on their land for two or more generations, making it all the more difficult for the Interior Department to carry out the Court's ruling. Resultant lawsuits and delays held up resolution of the matter, and the issue dragged on for several years. In 1921, Secretary of the Interior Albert Fall asked Senator Holm O. Bursum (who had replaced Fall in the U.S. Senate) to draft a bill to deal with the issue. It turned out that Bursum's bill was designed to give ownership to non-Indians who had held Indian land before 1902. Additionally, it was designed to cede to state courts (unsympathetic at the time to Indian grievances) jurisdiction to settle all other disputes relating to Indian land and water claims. When word got out that the bill was designed in favor of the non-Indian land-grabbers, it drew the indignation of a group of artists and writers from Taos who lobbied successfully to kill the measure. Finally, the Indian land rights issue was settled in 1924, when Congress passed the Pueblo Lands Act. That same year, Congress granted American citizenship to Indians born within the United States. However, it would be another twenty-four years before New Mexico granted Indians the right to vote.

Invasion of New Mexico

New Mexico was not yet five years in the Union when Columbus, a town of perhaps five hundred people close to the border with Mexico, was the scene of an invasion by a foreign military force. On the morning of March 9, 1916, legendary Mexican revolutionary leader

---

3. Ibid., p. 170.

Francisco "Pancho" Villa, leading a party of between nine hundred and a thousand Mexicans, staged an attack on the sleepy hamlet and nearby Camp Furlong, which was manned by a cavalry unit. The raid was in retaliation for President Woodrow Wilson's recognition of Venustiano Carranza (Villa's avowed enemy) as president of Mexico. During the assault, Villa's men shot out windows and ransacked stores, robbed and killed the owner and guests of the Commercial Hotel, and torched buildings before the cavalry chased them back into Mexico. Eighteen Americans died in the encounter and twelve were wounded. However, it was a costly raid for Villa, who lost 142 of his men.

The incursion brought swift retaliatory action from the United States. President Wilson sent an armed force of more than six thousand troops under General John "Black Jack" Pershing deep into Mexico in pursuit of Villa. Pershing's force did not catch up with Villa, but it inflicted many civilian casualties in the pursuit, further eroding relations between the two countries.[4]

POLITICS AND POLITICAL LEADERS SINCE STATEHOOD

Considering its chaotic and protracted struggle in achieving statehood, New Mexico has enjoyed a relatively unruffled political experience in the years since being admitted to the Union. Two months before President Taft signed the statehood bill, New Mexicans had already chosen their first state officeholders. The election on November 7, 1911, followed a hard-fought campaign. While the Republicans were in the majority at the time, the Democrats succeeded in capturing some key seats. The newly elected governor, William C. McDonald of Lincoln County, was a Democrat, as was Ezequiel C. de Baca of San Miguel County, who was elected lieutenant governor. However, the Republicans managed to win control of the legislature and a majority of seats on the state supreme court. Winning control of the state legislature gave the Republicans the opportunity to select New Mexico's first two U.S. senators. The honors went to Thomas B. Catron of Santa Fe and Albert B. Fall of Otero County, both staunch

---

4.   Fugate and Fugate, pp. 409–410.

Thomas B. Catron, c. 1917. (PHOTO BY WESLEY BRADFIELD)

Republicans. Catron was born near Lexington, Missouri, in 1840. He moved in 1866 to Las Cruces, New Mexico, where he practiced law, specializing in old Spanish and Mexican land grants. In the process he made himself one of the largest landowners in New Mexico and rose to be a dominant figure in the territory's Republican party ranks. He "wrote the party's platforms, controlled its conventions, represented it in national conventions and was a member of the Republican National Committee."[5] Upon New Mexico's admission into the Union as a state, he was rewarded with a seat in the United States Senate, serving there from 1912 to 1917. Albert Bacon Fall was born in Frankfort, Kentucky, in 1861. He also practiced law in Las Cruces. When New Mexico was admitted into the Union in 1912, he was the other Republican rewarded with a seat in the United States Senate. He served there until March 1921, when he resigned to accept a cabinet position in President Harding's administration. His political career ended in disgrace for his role in the oil leasing scandals of the early 1920s with oil tycoon Edward L. Doheny and others in Elk Hills, California, and Teapot Dome, Wyoming.

It would be the last time senators would be chosen by the state legislature. The power to do so would pass to the voters in 1913, with the passing of the Seventeenth Amendment to the United States Constitution. Each of the major parties won their share of the races for governor between 1912 and 1930. Governor McDonald served one four-year term; governors after that were limited to two consecutive, two-year terms. Ezequiel C. de Baca won election to the first two-year term in 1916, becoming the state's first Hispanic governor. De Baca died shortly after taking office, and the lieutenant governor, Republican Washington E. Lindsey of Roosevelt County, filled the vacancy. Lindsey had been a Roosevelt progressive and at the constitutional convention had advocated a number of progressive measures and electoral reforms that were vigorously opposed by the old-guard Republicans. His sponsorship of measures such as the direct primary and woman's suffrage also put him at odds with New Mexico's Spanish Americans and the influential commercial interests supporting the

---

5.   Beck, p. 301.

Republicans.[6] Because of his progressive stance, Lindsey became unacceptable to his party and as a result failed to win re-nomination. He was followed in the gubernatorial seat by Republican Octaviano A. Larrazolo, an outstanding Spanish-American leader and gifted public speaker. Larrazolo was once a Democratic candidate for the territorial governorship but had joined the Republican Party in 1911, believing its policies were more sensitive to the needs of the Spanish-speaking constituency.[7] Larrazolo proved to be as difficult for the Republican old guard as Lindsey had been. The liberal program he espoused was similar in many respects to that of his predecessor; moreover, he advocated expanding bilingual instruction, free textbooks, and other measures that would enhance the state's Spanish-American school curriculum. Larrazolo also became a casualty of the Republican old guard, which refused to support his re-nomination. The choice went instead to Judge Merritt C. Mechem, who was successful in retaining the governor's seat for the Republicans.

Two years later in 1922, the Democrats recaptured the gubernatorial seat when James Hinkle of Roswell won an easy victory over the Republican nominee, Dr. Charles L. Hill of Los Cruces. The Hinkle administration caused discord among the Democrats, and Hinkle was replaced as the Democratic nominee in 1924 by Arthur T. Hannett of Gallup. Hinkle's main source of unpopularity arose over the complaint that he had discriminated against Spanish Americans by not giving them a fair share of the choice patronage jobs.[8] Among those who assailed him was the maverick Republican turned Democratic, Bronson Cutting. Cutting, the publisher of the powerful Santa Fe *New Mexican*, had a large and loyal following in the Spanish-speaking community, where he was affectionately dubbed "El Don" by his supporters. He fought their battles, obtained jobs for them, attended their social functions, and was one of the few Anglos to be completely accepted by them.

The 1924 campaign was bitterly contested, and personal insults and accusations on both sides were extremely nasty. Although Hannett

---

6. Ibid., p. 304.
7. Ibid., p. 305.
8. Ibid., p. 306.

was depicted as a "wide-eyed radical only a few steps from Moscow,"[9] he won, albeit by a margin of fewer than two hundred votes. Cutting had thrown his support to Hannett and without question had helped him win. Their political partnership, however, began to disintegrate when Cutting discovered that the governor was using patronage to build up a political organization staffed by his own trustworthy supporters. But the real rift came about over a proposal to reform the state's election laws. In his inaugural address, Hannett had called attention to the shortcomings in existing state election laws and was pushing for remedial legislation to deal with such areas as voter registration, voting for the office instead of a straight party ticket, using a pen instead of a pencil to mark the ballot, and precluding anyone except the voter from marking the ballot or entering the polling booth. Republicans opposed the new election measures, perceiving them as a threat to their manipulation of the Spanish-American vote.[10] Cutting, who always stood up as a champion of all that was right, sided with the Republicans, for he too feared that passage would weaken his influence on his Spanish-speaking supporters. For that reason, he returned to the Republican Party from which he had recently departed and worked vigorously to defeat the bill. Fearful of change and naturally distrustful of the Anglos, the Spanish speakers believed their friend Bronson Cutting when he told them this was a plot against them.[11]

With the Republican feuding factions marching in concert again, a search was launched for a candidate capable of winning the 1926 gubernatorial election. They found such a man in Richard Dillon, who, with the support of Cutting and the Spanish Americans, succeeded in beating Hannett. Two years later he achieved the distinction of becoming the first governor to win reelection, although that distinction was marred by the fact that he presided over the collapse of the state's Republican Party. Beneath the surface the Cutting progressives and the old guard quarreled continuously for control of the party, but the issue that spelled disaster was establishing a state labor commissioner, which the Republican platform had promised.

---

9.   Ibid.
10. Beck, p. 309.
11. Ibid.

Cutting had unsuccessfully advocated for such a post during the Hannett administration and was again pushing the issue. Distrustful of Cutting's motives, the party leaders opted to renege on their campaign promise. Cutting was not pleased. Governor Dillon's gratitude to Cutting was recognized in 1927, when he appointed him to the vacancy in the U.S. Senate resulting from the death of Democratic Senator Andrieus A. Jones. The maverick Republican, who had never before held office, was elected to a full term the following year in the sweep that elected Herbert Hoover as president. He served in the Senate until his death in a plane crash in 1935. In spite of his Republican affiliation, Cutting supported Democrats when it was to his advantage. In 1930, he threw his support to the Democrats in the state elections that elected their candidate, Arthur Seligman. In the presidential election year of 1932, Cutting refused to support Hoover for reelection and instead supported Franklin D. Roosevelt; in many respects he was more radical than the New Dealers.[12] Cutting's hold on the Spanish American voters was so all-embracing that there is little doubt he took many of them into the Democratic ranks.

New Mexico's United States senators became their state's foremost politicians, particularly as the state came to depend more and more on federal funding. Many U.S. representatives aspired to be senators, yet only three of them made it—Chavez, Anderson, and Montoya. Some governors tried and none succeeded, at least by election. Dennis Chavez followed Bronson Cutting as one of the most dominant figures in New Mexico politics for many years.[13] In 1935, Chavez was appointed by Governor Clyde Tingley to the vacant seat created by the tragic death of Senator Cutting in a plane crash while returning to Washington, D.C. He went on to serve in the Senate for twenty-seven years, and he is memorialized as New Mexico's lone entry, at least for the time, in the Capitol's Statuary Hall. Throughout his career in Congress, Chavez made the most of his time working for the benefit of the people of New Mexico. He was a firm New Dealer who supported President Franklin D. Roosevelt and most of the president's

12. Larry Calloway, "Each Governor Left Own Legacy," *Albuquerque Journal,* September 19, 1999.

13. Beck, p. 314.

U.S. Senator Dennis Chavez. (PHOTO BY JOHN LeROUGE MARTINEZ)

legislative programs. He supported the Home Owner Loan Corporation, which allowed thousands of homeowners to keep their property. In the 1960s, when he served as chairman of the Senate Appropriations Subcommittee for Defense, he secured for New Mexico important defense-technology contracts, the most important stimuli for economic growth in the state for the next thirty years. Senator Chavez died in office in November 1962. Edwin Mechem, the governor at the time, resigned his office and appointed himself to the Senate seat. Two years later, Congressman Joseph M. Montoya defeated Mechem, moving up to the Senate. Democrat Montoya remained in the Senate until 1976, when he was defeated by astronaut Harrison Schmitt. Republican Schmitt served only one term when Jeff Bingaman captured the seat for the Democrats. Carl Hatch, U.S. senator from 1933 to 1948, tended to ignore state politics, concentrating on his duties in Washington. He was a consistent New Deal liberal, and his most notable accomplishment was the Hatch Act, which limits the partisan political activity former federal employees. In 1949 he was appointed United States district judge for the district of New Mexico and served until his retirement in 1963. Clinton P. Anderson served as a congressman from 1941 to 1945, as secretary of agriculture from 1945 to 1948, and from 1948 to 1972 as U.S. senator. He emerged as one of the nation's outstanding statesmen, particularly important for his work on the Atomic Energy Commission. Pete V. Domenici, when first elected to the U.S. Senate in 1972, was the first Republican from New Mexico to be elected to that body since Bronson Cutting in the early 1930s.

Throughout the 1930s and 1940s, the Democrats held on to the governor's seat. Predictably, New Mexican politics were not equally divided. The first five legislatures were Republican. In 1923 and again in 1925, the state Senate was captured by the Republicans, while the House went Democratic. From 1927 through 1931, both houses went Republican, revealing a definite preference for the Grand Old Party, From then on, Spanish-American voter support began to swing from the Republicans to the Democrats. Population shifts after 1930 were also partly responsible for the decline of the Republican Party; many Texans were migrating into eastern New Mexico, and more often than not, they were Democrats. Twenty years of uninterrupted tenure in the statehouse by the Democrats came to an end in 1950, when Republican Edwin L. Mechem was elected governor. He served four two-year terms over twelve years. Mechem's accomplishments did not benefit the Republican Party as a whole as the Democrats retained control of the state legislature and other state offices for much of the time.

Democrat Jack M. Campbell, a former agent of the Federal Bureau of Investigation, served as governor from 1963 to 1967. A conservative, Campbell is given credit for strengthening a law that provided for a nonpartisan civil service for state government, thereby ending a political patronage system that resulted in most rank-and-file state workers losing their jobs when a new governor took office. He was followed by David F. Cargo, a maverick Republican legislator from Albuquerque. Cargo had difficulty accomplishing anything in the Democratic legislature, but he did bring the movie industry to New Mexico. He was forced to call out the National Guard to deal with civil disturbances—the Rio Arriba County courthouse raid by land-grant followers of Reies Lopez Tijerina and, later, to quell anti-Vietnam rioting at the University of New Mexico.[14] Democrat Bruce King, a rancher, won his first term in 1970, succeeding Cargo. He served as governor intermittently for twelve years between 1971 and 1995. He was a masterful politician with a talent for remembering names and kept in touch with the people. With the help of Senator Pete Domenici, he lured Intel and its satellites to the Rio Rancho area. In 1994, Gary Johnson challenged King and won. Johnson's reelection in 1998 made him the first governor to serve consecutive four-year terms under a constitutional amendment. Bill Richardson was elected governor of New Mexico in 2002 by the largest margin of any candidate since 1964. Prior to that, Richardson had served for fifteen years as a congressman from New Mexico's 3rd Congressional District. He served as U.S. ambassador to the United Nations and as secretary of the U.S. Department of Energy during the Clinton administration.

The source of Republican strength in the early days of statehood came from the Spanish-American voters and the skills of several

---

14. Larry Calloway, "Each Governor Left Own Legacy," *Albuquerque Journal*, September 19, 1999.

colorful leaders whose control of the Republican Party was virtually undisputed. Typical of the early Republican political leaders were Thomas B. Catron and Albert B. Fall (discussed earlier in the chapter).[15] Although women generally expressed an interest in state politics, it was not until after the passage of the Nineteenth Amendment to the U.S. Constitution in 1920 that they could vote and hold elective office. Several women became actively involved in government. Among them was Lola Chavez de Armijo, who campaigned for the right of women to hold appointive office in the new state government. Soledad Chacon served as New Mexico's first female secretary of state. First elected in 1922, she won reelection in 1924 and then served as acting governor for a time in 1924, the first female to sit in the governor's chair.

DEPRESSION ERA

New Mexicans were not immediately affected by the Depression as it swept across the nation in the 1930s.[16] The reason, according to various sources, was that New Mexico was already an impoverished area when the Depression set in. At the end of the 1920s, while most of the United States was basking in an economic upswing, New Mexico remained one of the most deprived states in the nation, with one of the country's highest unemployment and illiteracy rates. A third of the families in rural New Mexico were living on less than one hundred dollars a year.

According to Professor María E. Montoya of the University of Michigan, there was relatively little industry, with the exception of extractive industries such as coal mining. There was no large-scale agriculture on which to base an expanding economy. Montoya writes:

> New Mexico languished in a colonial state, with entrepreneurs shipping the region's raw materials to the east. . . . Much of the state's land and property was controlled by the

---

15. Beck p. 300.
16. María E. Montoya, "Dennis Chavez and the Making of Modern New Mexico," in Richard W. Etulain (ed.), *New Mexican Lives*, p. 247.

federal government or eastern and European investors. Since United States occupation and conquest in 1848, New Mexicans had slowly been losing their land base to Anglos and other outsiders. . . . While politicians such as Senator Bronson Cutting had been successful in bringing federal dollars to the state, others, such as Senator Albert Fall, associated with the Teapot Dome scandal, had brought little but disrepute to the state. Consequently, New Mexico had never mustered a powerful congressional delegation in Washington that could work together for the benefit of the state.[17]

Ironic as it may seem, the Depression turned out to be a defining moment for New Mexico because President Roosevelt's New Deal channeled large amounts of much-needed funding to help the state's economic development. The New Deal spawned a myriad of national programs. Among them were the Agriculture Adjustment Act and the Taylor Grazing Act, which benefited the state immensely. Other programs, such as the Works Projects Administration and the Civilian Conservation Corps, focused on easing unemployment and poverty by providing job training to New Mexico's youth. Funding was also provided to revive Hispaño and Pueblo Indian culture and arts. Potters and weavers from the Rio Grande Pueblos, as well as Hispaño *santeros* and weavers, were paid to rediscover and work in their historic arts and crafts. Professional artists and up-and-coming artisans were likewise afforded employment to perform their skills during the lean years of the Depression. As New Mexico already had a national reputation in the art world, it was an ideal place to experiment with reviving the traditional arts and crafts.

WORLD WAR II AND ECONOMIC RECOVERY

From 1940 to the end of the century, New Mexico experienced a transformation in its economy and its lifestyle as far-reaching as that

---

17. María E. Montoya, "Dennis Chavez and the Making of Modern New Mexico," in Richard W. Etulain (ed.), *New Mexican Lives*, pp. 248–249.

brought about by the arrival of the Spaniards and, later, the Americans. The impetus for the change, as in earlier times, came from the outside.[18] The war years, from 1940 to 1945, marked the expansion of the federal government in the state, launching a military presence that exists still today. In the late 1930s, with economic recovery already on the upswing, national defense found New Mexico's excellent weather, vast open spaces, and centrally located emerging urban areas attractive for military training and weapons research. In 1943, the isolated area of Los Alamos became the site for the top-secret project to develop the atomic bomb, turning New Mexico into a center for some of the most important nuclear research and development in the nation. Many of the developments begun under the pressures of war did not disappear once the conflict had ended. Not only did many of the newly created installations become permanent, but some existing ones grew rapidly and merged with others. The federal investment in New Mexico also produced its own economic environment as a new population created a greater local market for products.[19] It was at this time that New Mexico's economy (at least in the Rio Grande valley from Los Alamos and Santa Fe down to Doña Ana County and White Sands) began its makeover from agrarian to industrial. In World War II, New Mexicans demonstrated their patriotism and loyalty to the United States by fulfilling their obligations to the war effort. Montoya writes that men from New Mexico left their homes to fight on both the Pacific and European war fronts. Two of their regiments were at Bataan in the Philippines, and, after Bataan fell to the Japanese, they endured the infamous "Death March" and years of imprisonment. Mexican Americans in general, and New Mexicans in particular, stood out among American soldiers. In fact, the state distinguished itself by the number of Congressional Medals of Honor awarded per capita.[20] One group of New Mexicans, the Navajo code breakers, played a unique role in the war effort. When the Japanese military was intercepting Allied messages and creating confusion with deceptive information, Navajo

---

18. Tobias, p. 171.
19. Ibid., P. 172.
20. María E. Montoya, "Dennis Chavez and the Making of Modern New Mexico," in Etulain, p. 254.

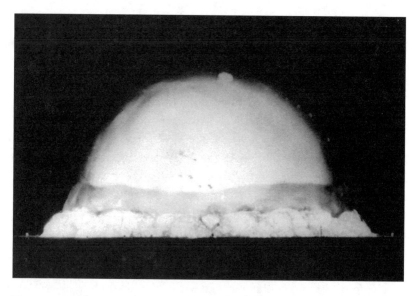

First atomic blast at White Sands, NM, July 16, 1945.

Inspecting and testing after the atomic blast, Trinity Site, White Sands, NM, c. 1946.

Indians, under the guidance of the military, perfected a special code using their native language, which the Japanese could not decode.

POSTWAR PROGRESS

Significant economic changes occurred in Mexico following World War II. At Los Alamos in 1943, the federal government sealed off a tract of land on the Pajarito Plateau west of Santa Fe and built the Los Alamos National Laboratory to carry out the "Manhattan Project." Under the direction of Robert Oppenheimer, and later Norris E. Bradbury, a team of scientists and scores of support staff lived and worked in almost complete seclusion, developing the world's first nuclear weapons, the first of which was tested at the Trinity Site, north of White Sands in southern New Mexico on July 16, 1945.

With the coming of the Korean War and then the Cold War, New Mexico's economy continued its upward surge. White Sands Missile Range continued as a testing ground for rocket development and lunar probes; today it is one of America's most important astrophysics sites. Aerospace research and defense contracts are economic mainstays in Albuquerque. Los Alamos continues to be a national leader in nuclear technology, while Kirtland Air Force Base is the home of the Air Force Special Weapons Center. The International Space Hall of Fame in Alamogordo honors the men and women who have committed their lives to space exploration.

The federal government is the largest employer in the state. Many government jobs are related to the military; there are several air force bases, along with national observatories and the Los Alamos and Sandia laboratories. A high-technology industry, much of it linked to national security, has become increasingly important to the state's economy. New Mexico, moreover, is a state rich in natural resources, and much of the state's income is derived from its mineral wealth, which includes considerable quantities of uranium, manganese, potash, copper, natural gas, beryllium, and tin. Tourism is also an important source of income, and the federal government maintains the unspoiled beauty and natural wonders of the state's national forests and monuments.

Best known are the Carlsbad Caverns National Park and the Aztec Ruins National Monument, which attract thousands of tourists annually. Other attractions include the White Sands, Bandelier, Capulin Volcano, El Morro, Fort Union, Gila Cliff Dwellings, Salinas Pueblo Missions, and Chaco Culture National Historical Park; Taos and other extant pueblos complete this list.

Paradoxically, growth has not been universally welcomed. Many New Mexicans worry that lack of water resources in the dry Southwest will eventually restrain population growth. Warnings that surface water and underground aquifers are being too rapidly allocated intensifies the debate between advocates of growth and environmentalists who fear significant damage to the fragile desert ecosystems.

Things Cultural

New Mexico has attracted men and women of artistic expression who hail from other places. Today, as in the past, these artists (writers and painters) draw inspiration from the beauty of the landscape and are influenced by the fusion of the state's three divergent cultures—Indian, Spanish, and Anglo. In the words of Warren A. Beck:

> The original Indian civilization was blended with that of the Hispanic, but the Spaniards were in turn deeply influenced by the Indians with whom they came in contact. This distinctive civilization was, in its turn, modified by the impact of the Anglos during the nineteenth century. But just as the Spaniards were influenced by the Indians, so also have the Anglos been greatly affected by the culture they found in New Mexico.[21]

Among the authors influenced by New Mexico who later attained distinction were D. H. Lawrence, Adolph Francis Bandelier, Maxwell Anderson, Alice Corbin, Mary Austin, Willa Cather, Witter Bynner,

---

21. Beck, p. 316.

Taos Pueblo. (PHOTO BY CLAIRE MATHER)

Ghost Ranch Living Museum located in Carson National Forest. (PHOTO BY CLAIRE MATHER)

Queen's Room, Carlsbad Caverns, NM. (PHOTO BY RAY V. DAVIS)

Paul Horgan, and Harvey and Erna Fergusson. Much of the litera-
ture on New Mexico concerns the Indians, and among those who
studied and wrote of their tribal organization and culture was Mary
Austin. A secondary theme to that of the Indian way of life is the
Anglo influence on the Spanish-American ethic. This theme is ably
presented in several of Harvey Fergusson's books. Perhaps the most
highly acclaimed work of fiction with a New Mexico setting is Willa
Cather's *Death Comes for the Archbishop*. This celebrated novel, while
primarily concerned with the problems of Bishop Lamy, his French
clergy, and their efforts to reform New Mexico's Catholic Church after
the territory was acquired by the United States, also contains valuable
information about early customs and local traditions in New Mexico.
Mabel Dodge, a wealthy New Yorker, did a great deal to promote New
Mexico as a site for artistic expression. She moved west, founded
a colony of writers alongside the art colony in Taos, and married
Pueblo Indian Tony Luhan. She invited writers from all over, among
whom was the famous English writer D. H. Lawrence, whose presence attracted other writers and artists to the Taos area. New Mexico
also attracted painters. Bert G. Phillips and Ernest L. Blumenschein
were among the first to arrive. Both men had studied painting in Paris
before arriving in Taos in 1898. They encouraged many artists to
move there and were influential in founding the Taos Society of Artists in 1915. Among the many painters identified with New Mexico
is native-born Peter Hurd, who developed his own style of painting,
"tempera on yeso," a technique related to his work as a muralist.[22]
Among the noted women painters who took their artistic talents to
New Mexico are Becky Strand and Georgia O'Keeffe. O'Keeffe arrived
in New Mexico in 1929 and painted canvases of her adopted homeland from her home in Abiquiu. O'Keeffe's canvases won national
acclaim and established her as one of America's greatest modern-day
women painters.[23] New Mexico's Indian painters gained fame as well.
Among them are Pablita Velarde, best known for her paintings and
murals in public buildings, and R. C. Gorman, whose paintings hang
in art galleries and private homes in many countries.

---

22. Fergusson, *Three People*, p. 378.
23. Ibid., p. 375.

The history of New Mexico is the story of the land and its people. Throughout its long history, this land along the Rio Grande has meant many things to many people. Few, however, have described the New Mexico experience more fittingly than native daughter Erna Fergusson, who wrote the following:

New Mexico is the scene of the longest span of human development in the Western Hemisphere. Traces of earliest man have been found in a mountain cave; on a high plateau the atomic bomb was made. Much of the long drama of human development has been only faintly reflected in New Mexico, but the acts that have been played here have left to the modern state vestiges of a pageant of three peoples. The rites of prehistoric Indians and of Europeans of the Middle Ages are still practiced here. The two frontiers—Spanish and United States—met and fused in New Mexico. This is important for the record. It is of greater value, now that our country has been forced into world leadership, that in New Mexico the peoples of three cultures have successfully worked out a life together.[24]

---

24. Ibid., p. xxi.

Chronology of
New Mexico History[1]

c. 25000 BC	People of an unknown type, described by archaeologists as Sandia people, leave earliest evidence of human existence in what is now New Mexico.
c. 10000–9000 BC	Clovis people, named for the site where artifacts established their presence, hunted the area in search of mammoth, bison, and other game.
c. 9000–8000 BC	Folsom people lived and hunted throughout the Southwest at the end of the last ice age.
c. 10000–500 BC	This is the period of the Cochise people, the link between the ancient mammoth hunters and later cultures, and the earliest inhabitants to cultivate corn, squash and beans.
c. 300 BC–AD 1200	The Mogollon people, the first post-Cochise era culture, created one-room pit-house villages in the mountains and produced pottery of fine quality.
c. 100 BC–AD 1300	Anasazi people, nicknamed basket makers, because of the delicate baskets they made from yucca fibers, first appeared at the Four Corners area. They had evolved into the highly developed Chaco Civilization before mysteriously disappearing in the 1300s.

---

1. Many sources were consulted in developing this timeline, chiefly from the following: www.ppsa.com/magazine/Nmtimeline.html.

AD 700–1050	Pueblo period unfolds: adobe houses, use of cotton cloth and infant cradle boards prevail.
1050–1300	Great Pueblo period is under way: multistoried pueblos, practice of irrigation and road systems prevail.
1000–1400	Navajos and Apaches migrate from the Great Plains into New Mexico
1100–1150	Hopis move into their mesa-top dwellings.
1492	Columbus discovers America.
1521	Cortés captures Mexico City.
1528	Narvaez lands in Florida in April; later that year, his party is shipwrecked. Cabeza de Vaca, Estéban the Moor, and two others survive and begin their seven-and-a-half-year journey.
1536	Cabeza de Vaca and his party reach Mexico City after crossing what is now southern New Mexico; they start rumors of the Seven Golden Cities of Cibola.
1539	Marcos de Niza, guided by Estéban the Moor, leads party northward from Culiacán, Mexico, in search of the Seven Cities of Cibola. They reach the Zuni village of Hawikuh in present-day New Mexico, where Estéban is killed.
1540–1542	Coronado leads an expedition north and captures a Zuni Indian pueblo at Hawikuh, believing it to be one of the legendary wealthy Seven Cities of Cibola.
1580–1581	Agustín Rodríguez leads an expedition to New Mexico; four members of the party are killed by Indians.
1582–1583	Bernadino Beltrán and Antonio de Espejo lead an expedition to New Mexico to search for survivors of the ill-fated Rodríguez mission.
1598	Juan de Oñate leads a party of colonists into New Mexico and establishes the first Spanish capital of San Juan de los Caballeros at the Tewa village of Ohke, north of present-day Española.
1599	Battle at Acoma occurs between natives and Spaniards; some six to eight hundred natives are killed, and many are taken prisoner.
1600	San Gabriel, second capital of New Mexico, is founded at the confluence of the Rio Grande and the Chama River.

1608	Oñate is removed as governor and sent to Mexico City to be tried for mistreatment of the Indians and abuse of power; decision is made by the Spanish Crown to continue settlement of New Mexico as a royal province.
1609–1610	Pedro de Peralta establishes a new capital at Santa Fe.
1626	The Spanish Inquisition is established in New Mexico.
1641	Luis de Rosas is assassinated by colonists during conflict between the church and state.
1675	Franciscans establish missions in Hopiland.
1680	The Pueblo Indian revolt takes place; surviving colonists flee to El Paso del Norte.
1692–1693	The reconquest of Santa Fe is undertaken by Diego de Vargas.
1696	A second Pueblo revolt is attempted; however, efforts are thwarted by Vargas.
1706	Albuquerque is founded.
1743	French trappers reach Santa Fe and begin limited trade with the Spanish.
1776	Franciscan friars Dominguez and Escalante explore a route from New Mexico to California.
1786	Bautista de Anza makes peace with the Comanche Indians.
1807	Pike leads first Anglo-American expedition into New Mexico; publishes account upon return to the United States.
1821	Mexico declares independence from Spain; Santa Fe Trail is opened to international trade.
1821–1848	New Mexico is part of the Republic of Mexico.
1834	Mission properties are escheated to the Mexican state.
1837	Chimayo Revolt against Mexican taxation leads to the assassination of Albino Pérez and top officials.
1841	Texas soldiers cross into New Mexico and claim all land east of the Rio Grande for Texas; the incursion is thwarted by Manuel Armijo.
1846	The Mexican-American War begins; Kearny annexes New Mexico to the United States.

1847	Taos Rebellion is carried out against the United States military; Charles Bent is killed.
1848	Treaty of Guadalupe Hidalgo ends the Mexican-American War.
1850	New Mexico (which then included present-day Arizona, southern Colorado, southern Utah, and southern Nevada) is designated a territory.
1851	Lamy arrives in New Mexico to take up the Santa Fe Roman Catholic diocese.
1854	The Gadsden Purchase adds forty-five thousand square miles to New Mexico.
1861	Texas Confederates invade New Mexico.
1862	Jefferson Davis signs act of Confederate Congress establishing the Territory of Arizona as part of the Confederacy.
1862	Battles of Valverde and Glorieta Pass bring an end to Confederate occupation of New Mexico.
1863	President Lincoln signs law partitioning New Mexico; Territory of Arizona is created.
1864	Kit Carson defeats the Navajos at Canyon de Chelly and removes them to the Bosque Redondo Reservation, where thousands die of disease and starvation before they are finally permitted to return to their homeland.
1878	The railroad arrives in New Mexico, opening full-scale trade and migration from the East and Midwest. Lincoln County War erupts in southeastern New Mexico.
1881	Billy the Kid is shot by Sheriff Pat Garrett at Fort Sumner.
1886	Geronimo, the legendary Chiricahua Apache war leader, surrenders, putting an end to Indian hostilities in the Southwest.
1910	New Mexico constitution is drafted in preparation for statehood.
1912	New Mexico is admitted to the Union as the forty-seventh state.
1916	Mexican revolutionary leader, Pancho Villa, invades New Mexico.

1922	Secretary of State Soledad Chacon and Superintendent of Public Instruction Isabel Eckles are the first women elected to statewide office.
1942–1945	World War II: the Japanese capture New Mexican soldiers and force them to endure the Bataan Death March; Navajo "code talkers" are vital to the war effort.
1943	Secret atomic laboratories are established at Los Alamos.
1945	World's first atomic bomb, developed at Los Alamos, is detonated at Trinity Site in southern New Mexico.
1948	Native Americans win the right to vote in state elections.
1966	New state capitol is dedicated.
1982	Space shuttle *Columbia* lands at White Sands Space Harbor near Alamogordo.
1998	New Mexico celebrates its *cuartocentenario*, or four-hundred-year anniversary, commemorating its 1598 founding by Juan de Oñate.

Glossary

adobe — Building material made from mixing clay and sand with water.

alcalde mayor — Local official during the Spanish period who acted as judge and handled local affairs.

apostate — Name Spaniards gave to a Pueblo Indian who left the Rio Grande valley during the 1700s; the apostates refused to obey Spanish rule and moved away from their homes.

cabildo — Town council during the Spanish period; members advised the governor about matters of concern to the people.

carreta — Wooden, two-wheeled cart used in New Mexico during Spanish and Mexican periods.

cibola — Spanish word that means "buffalo cow" and name applied to the area north of New Spain, which the Spaniards believed was very rich.

conquistador — Any Spaniard who conquered lands in the Americas for Spain.

custodio — Director of the Franciscan missionaries in a given area, such as New Mexico.

ciné — Navajo word meaning "people."

encomienda — System under which Spanish soldiers were given Indians to care for and oversee and in exchange received labor and tribute from the Indians.

hacendado — Hacienda owner; hacendados hired workers to farm their lands and care for their livestock.

hacienda	Large farm where both crops and livestock were raised; found in Spanish colonial New Mexico.
hogan	Traditional house of the Navajos.
horno	Dome-shaped, outdoor oven in which Indian and Hispanic women of New Mexico did their baking.
kachina	A supernatural being in the Pueblo Indian mythology or a messenger of a Pueblo Indian god; the word is also applied to dolls made in the image of the supernatural.
kiva	Religious center of the Anasazi and the Pueblo Indians and very important to the cultures whose religious ceremonies took place there.
mesa	A flat-topped area that rises above the surrounding land.
mestizo	Child of a Spaniard and an Indian.
pueblo	Spanish word that means "town"; also used to name the adobe houses of the Anasazi and the Indians and, when capitalized, to describe the Indians of New Mexico—Taos Pueblo, Zuni Pueblo, Hopi Pueblo, etc.
reservation	Land area set aside for Indians to live on.
royal colony	Colony under the direct control of the Spanish rulers; New Mexico was a Spanish royal colony beginning in 1609.
sedentary	Word used to describe a way of life in which a people settle down and build permanent homes.
shaman	Navajo or Apache medicine man; also in charge of religious rites.
viceroy	King or queen's agent in the New World; New Spain's highest-ranking official.

Bibliography

Albano, Bob (ed.). *Days of Destiny*. Phoenix: Arizona Highways, 1999.

Bancroft, Hubert H. *History of Arizona and New Mexico, 1530–1888*. San Francisco: The History Company, 1889.

Banks, Leo W., and Robert J. Farrell. *They Left Their Mark*. Wild West Collection, v. 3. Phoenix, AZ: Arizona Dept. of Transportation, 1997.

Bartlett, John. *Familiar Quotations*. 14th edition: Little, Brown and Company. Boston, MA, 1968.

Baxter, John O. *Las Carneradas: Sheep Trade in New Mexico, 1700–1860*. Albuquerque: University of New Mexico Press, 1987.

Beck, Warren A. *New Mexico: A History of Four Centuries*. Norman, OK: University of Oklahoma Press, 1977.

Calloway, Larry. "Each Governor Left Own Legacy," Albuquerque: *Albuquerque Journal,* September 19, 1999.

Cather, Willa. *Death Comes for the Archbishop*. New York: Vintage, 1990.

Cermony, John C. *Life among the Apaches*. Lincoln, NE: University of Nebraska Press, 1983.

Charles, Tom. *Story of the Great White Sands*. Alamogordo, NM: National Parks Service, 1948.

Cleveland, Agnes Morley. *No Life for a Lady*. Boston: Houghton Miffin, 1941.

Cooke, Philip St. George. *The Conquest of New Mexico and California in 1846–1848*. Chicago: Rio Grande Press, 1964.

Cordell, Linda. *Archaeology of the Southwest*. San Diego: Academic Press, 1997.

Corle, Edwin, *The Gila: River of the Southwest*. New York: Rinehart and Co., 1951.

Davis, Margaret Leslie. *Dark Side of Fortune*. Berkeley: University of California Press, 2001.

Davis, W. W. H. *El Gringo, or New Mexico and Her People*. Lincoln, NE: University of Nebraska Press, 1982.

Deutsch, Sarah J. *No Separate Refuge: Culture, Class, and Gender on an Anglo-Hispanic Frontier in the American Southwest, 1880–1940*. New York: Oxford University Press, 1987.

Estergreen, M. Morgan. *Kit Carson: A Portrait of Courage*. Norman, OK: University of Oklahoma Press, 1962.

Etulain, Richard W. (ed.). *Contemporary New Mexico, 1940–1990*. Albuquerque: University of New Mexico Press, 1994.

Etulain, Richard W. (ed.). *New Mexican Lives*. Albuquerque: University of New Mexico Press, 2002.

Fehrenbach, T. R. *The Comanches: Destruction of a People*. New York: Da Capo Press, 1994.

Ferguson, William M. *Anasazi Ruins of the Southwest*. Albuquerque: University of New Mexico Press, 1985.

Fergusson, Erna. *New Mexico: A Pageant of Three Peoples*. New York, Knopf, 1964.

———. *Our Southwest*. New York, Knopf, 1940.

Fierman, Floyd. *Roots and Boots: From Crypto-Jew in New Spain to Community Leader in the Southwest*. Hoboken, NJ: KTAV Publishing House, Inc., 1988

Fisher, David Hackett. *The Great Wave*. New York: Oxford University Press, 1996.

Forrest, Suzanne. *The Preservation of the Village: New Mexico's Hispanics and the New Deal*. Albuquerque: University of New Mexico Press, 1998.

French, Maurice. *The Frenchs of French Park*. Warminster, UK: Maurice French, 1999.

French, William. *Some Recollections of a Western Ranchman*. Silver City, NM: High-Lonesome Books, 1997.

Fugate, Francis, and Roberta Fugate. *Roadside History of New Mexico*. Missoula, MT: Mountain Press, 1998.

Gibson, Arrell Morgan. *The Santa Fe and Taos Colonies: Age of the Muses, 1900–1942*. Norman, OK: University of Oklahoma Press, 1988.

Goetzmann, William N. *Army Exploration in the American West, 1803–1863*. Austin: Texas State Historical Association, 1991.

Greenberg, Martin (ed.). *The Tony Hillerman Companion*. New York: Harper Collins, 1994.

Gregg, Andrew K. *New Mexico in the Nineteenth Century*. Austin: Eakin Press, 1968.

Gregg, Josiah (ed. by Milo Milton Quaife). *The Commerce of the Prairies*. New York: Citadel Press, Inc., 1968.

Griswold del Castillo, R. *The Treaty of Guadalupe Hidalgo: A Legacy of Conflict*. Norman, OK: University of Oklahoma Press, 1990.

Harris, Richard. *Hidden New Mexico*. Berkeley: Ulysses Press, 1997.

Hillerman, Tony (ed.). *The Best of the West: An Anthology of Classic Writing from the American West*. New York: Harper, 1991.

Horgan, Paul. *Great River: Rio Grande in North American History*. Middletown, CT: Wesleyan University Press, 1991.

Hyde, George E. (ed. by Savoie Lottinvile). *Life of George Bent Written from His Letters*. Norman, OK: University of Oklahoma Press, 1983.

Josephy, Alvin M. *The Civil War in the American West*. New York: Knopf, 1991.

Keleher, William A. *Violence in Lincoln County: 1869–1881*. Albuquerque: University of New Mexico Press, 1982.

Kelly, Lawrence C. *The Assault on Assimilation: John Collier and the Origins of Indian Policy Reform*. Albuquerque: Olympic Marketing Corp, 1983.

Kerby, Robert Lee. *The Confederate Invasion of New Mexico and Arizona, 1861–1862*. Los Angeles: Westernlore Publications, 1958.

Knaut, Andrew L. *The Pueblo Revolt of 1680*. Norman, OK: University of Oklahoma Press, 1995.

Lamar, Howard Roberts. *The Far Southwest, 1846–1912: A Territorial History*. Albuquerque: University of New Mexico Press, 2000.

Larson, Robert W. *New Mexico's Quest for Statehood, 1846–1912*. Albuquerque: University of New Mexico Press, 1968.

Lavin, Patrick. *Arizona: An Illustrated History*. New York: Hippocrene, 2001.

Lister, Florence, and Robert Lister. *Those Who Came Before*. Tucson: Southwest Parks and Monuments Association, 1983.

Lockwood, Frank P. *The Apache Indians*. Lincoln, NE: University of Nebraska Press, 1987.

McCarty, John L. *Maverick Town: The Story of Old Tascosa*. Norman, OK: University of Oklahoma Press, 1968.

McDougall, Walter. *The Heavens and the Earth: A Political History of the Space Age*. Baltimore: The John Hopkins University Press, 1997.

Merk, Frederick. *Manifest Destiny and Mission in American History: A Reinterpretation*. New York: Vintage Press, 1966.

Metz, Leon C. *Pat Garrett: The Story of a Western Lawman*. Norman, OK: University of Oklahoma Press, 1987.

Murphy, Lawrence. *Philmont: A History of New Mexico's Cimarron County*. Albuquerque: University of New Mexico Press, 1976.

Nash, Gerald D. *The American West in the Twentieth Century: A Short History of an Urban Oasis*. Albuquerque: University of New Mexico Press, 1977.

Nugent, Walter. *Into the West*. New York: Vintage Press, 2001.

Opler, Morris E. *Apache Odyssey: A Journey between Two Worlds*. New York: Holt, Rinehart and Winston, 1969.

Osgood, Ernest S. *Day of the Cattleman*. Chicago: University of Chicago Press, 1993.

Otero, Miguel Antonio. *My Nine Years as Governor of the Territory of New Mexico, 1897–1906*. Santa Fe: Sunstone Press, 2000.

Page, Jake. *In the Hands of the Great Spirit*. New York: Free Press, 2003.

Riketts, Norma B. *The Mormon Battalion: U.S. Army of the West, 1846–1848*. Logan, UT: Utah State University Press, 1996.

Roberts, Calvin A., and Susan A. Roberts. *A History of New Mexico*. Albuquerque: University of New Mexico Press, 1998).

Rothman, Hal K. *Preserving Different Pasts: The American National Monuments*. Urbana, IL: University of Illinois Press, 1989.

Santiago, Mark. *The Red Captain: The Life of Hugo O'Conor*. Tucson: Arizona Historical Society, 1994.

Seagraves, Anne. *High-Spirited Women of the West*. Hayden, ID: Treasure Chest Books, 1992.

Secor-Welsh, Cynthia. Introduction. *My Life on the Frontier, 1864–1882*. By Miguel Antonio Otero. Albuquerque: University of New Mexico Press, 1987.

Sheridan, Thomas E. *Arizona: A History*. Tucson: University of Arizona Press, 1995.

———. *A History of the Southwest*. Tucson: Western National Parks Association, 1998.

Shumatoff, Alex. *Legends of the American Desert*. New York: HarperPerennial, 1999.

Silverberg, Robert. *The Pueblo Revolt*. Lincoln, NE: University of Nebraska Press, 1994.

Simmons, Marc. *The Last Conquistador: Don Juan de Oñate and the Settling of the Far Southwest*. Norman, OK: University of Oklahoma Press, 1993.

———. *New Mexico: An Interpretive History*. Albuquerque: University of New Mexico Press, 1988.

Smith, Toby. *Odyssey*. Albuquerque: University of New Mexico Press, 1987.

Spicer, Edward H. *Cycles of Conquest*. Tucson: University of Arizona Press, 1997.

Sweeney, Edwin R. *Mangas Coloradas*. Norman, OK: University of Oklahoma Press, 1998.

Thrapp, Dan F. *Conquest of Apacheria*. Norman, OK: University of Oklahoma Press, 1979.

Tobias, Henry, *A History of the Jews in New Mexico*. Albuquerque: University of New Mexico Press, 1990.

Trager, James. *The People's Chronology*. New York: Holt, 1992.

Trimble, Marshall. *Roadside History of Arizona*. Missoula, MT: Mountain Press Publishing Company, 1986.

Tyler, Daniel A. *Concise History of the Mormon Battalion in the Mexican War, 1846–1847*. Whitefish, MT: Kessinger Publishing LLC, 1964.

Utley, Robert M. *Billy the Kid*. New York: Tauris Parke, 1989.

———. *High Noon in Lincoln*. Albuquerque: University of New Mexico Press, 1998.

Weber, David J. *The Spanish Frontier in North America*. New Haven: Yale University Press, 1992.

Weinberg, Albert K., *Manifest Destiny: A Study of Nationalist Expansion in American History*. Victoria, BC: Peter Smith Publishing, 1963.

Index

About the Author

Patrick Lavin was born in Ireland. An avid history enthusiast, he spends his retirement years researching and writing historical books and articles. His published works include *Celtic Ireland West of the River Shannon* (2003), *Arizona: An Illustrated History* (Hippocrene Books, 2001), *The Celtic World: An Illustrated History 700 BC to the Present* (Hippocrene Books, 1999), and *Thank You Ireland* (1994). Patrick is a graduate of California State University, Northridge, and is retired from a career with the federal government. He currently makes his home in Tucson, Arizona.

Also available from Hippocrene Books . . .

ILLUSTRATED HISTORIES

Arizona: An Illustrated History
Patrick Lavin

From prehistory through the Spanish conquest and the "wild west," here is the complete illustrated history of Arizona, the Grand Canyon State. Patrick Lavin explores the "land of contrasts," whose history is as varied and fascinating as its landscapes. No other North American region offers such environmental diversity, including the native plants, animals, and people that inhabit it. Complemented by over 60 photographs and maps, this concise history recounts the story of the state from the prehistoric days of the Paleo-Indians to the twenty-first century.

225 pages • 5 x 7 • 0-7818-0852-9 • $14.95pb • (102)

California: An Illustrated History
Robert J. Chandler

California: An Illustrated History, complete with over 70 pictures and maps, is the perfect introduction to the events and people that have shaped this great state. Robert J. Chandler's sweeping history begins with the area's indigenous inhabitants, and leads through the era of Spanish colonization, conquest by the United States, the gold rush, the founding of Hollywood, and the present.

252 pages • 5½ x 8½ • 0-7818-1034-5 • $14.95pb • (583)

Florida: An Illustrated History
Robert A. Taylor

From Spanish conquistadors to Jeb Bush—the grand history of Florida is presented here with over 50 illustrations, photographs, and maps. This volume traces Florida's evolution from European colony to American state. It chronicles the struggles between the United States and Spain, the trauma of the Civil War, and the ways Floridians have grappled with the problems of over-development in the "Sunshine State." Perfect for the vacationer, student, or curious reader.

238 pages • 5½ x 8½ • 0-7818-1052-3 • $14.95pb • (36)

Missouri: An Illustrated History

Sean McLachlan

Here is a lively and thorough account of pivotal events in Missouri's history—including Spanish and French settlement, the Civil War era, the age of jazz and prohibition, twentieth-century labor and civil rights struggles, and the dawn of a new century. This volume features fascinating material from diaries, newspaper articles, journals, and letters of ordinary Missourians; analysis of Missouri's changing economy, geography, industries, and immigrant populations; and 80 b/w photos, illustrations, and maps.

275 pages • 5½ x 8½ • 0-7818-1196-5 • $14.95pb • (333)

Virginia: An Illustrated History

Deborah Welch

With over 60 photographs, illustrations and maps, *Virginia: An Illustrated History* guides readers through a concise, intriguing look at Virginia's crucial role in American history.

The seeds of an American nation were planted in Jamestown, Virginia, and from that moment, Virginia's history became inextricably linked to the birth of a new nation. Sons of Virginia led the revolt against the British, drafted The Declaration of Independence, and helmed the Confederate side of the civil war. Modern-day Virginians from Arthur Ashe to Douglas Wilder, the first African-American governor in American history, broke new ground for racial equality. Virginia reflects the complex history, breathtaking beauty, and the unsurpassed potential of America itself.

220 pages • 5½ x 8½ • 0-7818-1115-5 • $14.95pb • (375)

TRAVEL GUIDES

The Navajo Nation: A Visitor's Guide
Patrick and Joan Lavin

Navajoland spans sections of Arizona, New Mexico, and southern Utah, and is home to numerous sites of historical interest and spectacular natural beauty. This handy volume covers attractions, accommodations, and scenic routes, and includes a guide to hiking and camping as well as 16-page color photo insert. In addition to serving as a travel guide, the book also explores the history, culture, language, and religion of the Navajo people.

288 pages • 5½ x 8½ • 0-7818-1180-5 • $21.95pb • (54)

Discover Native America: Arizona, Colorado, New Mexico & Utah, Second Edition
Tish Minear and Janet Limon

This new edition of a popular Hippocrene travel guide highlights the cultures, languages, and histories of modern tribes, including the Navajo, Apache, Ute, Tohono O'odham, Pueblo, and Hopi—populating the spectacular "Four Corners" area of the American Southwest. This area encompasses the Colorado Plateau and extends from central New Mexico to southern Nevada, Utah, and Arizona. Arranged geographically, the guide includes: tips on visiting reservations, attending ceremonies, and buying arts and crafts; dozens of new sites and places to stay, eat, and shop; calendars of powwows and other tribal ceremonies; maps and 16-page color photo insert.

455 pages • 6 x 9 • 0-7818-1198-9 • $24.95pb • (338)

LANGUAGE TITLES

Instant Spanish Vocabulary Builder with CD
Tom Means

Many words in Spanish are nearly the same as their English counterparts, except for the word ending. This unique book identifies the 24 most common word-ending patterns between these languages and provides over 4,000 words that follow them. Perfect as a classroom supplement or for self-study, it is appropriate for all ages and levels of experience. The enclosed CD allows the reader to master pronunciation of the most common words and phrases from each chapter by repeating them after a native speaker.

209 pages • 6 x 9 • 0-7818-0981-9 • $14.95pb • (338)

Spanish-English / English-Spanish Compact Dictionary (Latin American)
Ila Warner

- Concise and portable
- Side-by-side pronunciation
- 3,700 total dictionary entries
- Brief guide to Spanish grammar and pronunciation
- Ideal for travelers, students, and businesspeople

170 pages • 3 x 4½ • 0-7818-1041-8 • $8.95pb • (649)

Spanish-English / English-Spanish (Latin American) Concise Dictionary
Ila Warner

- Over 8,000 word-to-word entries
- Phonetic pronunciation in both languages
- An informative guide to Spanish pronunciation
- A concise, easy-to-use format
- Completely modern and up-to-date entries
- A list of culinary terms from Spanish-speaking countries

310 pages • 4 x 6 • 0-7818-0261-X • $12.95pb • (258)

COOKBOOKS

Aprovecho: A Mexican-American Border Cookbook
Teresa Cordero-Cordell and Robert Cordell

Aprovecho, which means "I make best use of," is a celebration of the food and culture found along the U.S.-Mexico border. This comprehensive book contains more than 250 recipes, including such traditional fare as enchiladas, quesadillas, and margaritas, along with more exotic delights, such as Cactus Salad, Lobster and Tequila, and Watermelon Sorbet. In addition to appetizing recipes, this entertaining cookbook contains special sections that relate popular legends, explain how tequila is made, and provide instructions for making your own festive piñatas. Also included are a glossary of chiles and cooking terms as well as a Mexican pantry list so you'll always be prepared for a fiesta!

PB: 377 pages • 6 x 9 • 978-0-7818-1206-1 • $16.95 • (428)
HC: 377 pages • 6 x 9 • 978-0-7818-1026-4 • $24.95 • (554)

Mexican Culinary Treasures: Recipes from Maria Elena's Kitchen
Maria Elena Cuervo-Lorens

This cookbook provides insight into modern Mexican cooking and the history behind it. The recipes range from very traditional dishes like tacos to the modern cuisine of Mexico City such as chicken in prune and red wine sauce. Maria Elena Cuervo-Loren's extensive knowledge of the nation's culinary traditions combined with an enthusiasm for sharing the vibrant flavors of her native Mexico make this book a fascinating journey through Mexico's culinary treasures.

266 pages • 6 x 9 • 0-7818-1061-2 • $24.95hc • (107)

Prices subject to change without prior notice. To purchase Hippocrene Books contact your local bookstore, call (718) 454-2366, or visit www.hippocrenebooks.com.